The Illustrated Book of Development Definitions

by Harvey S. Moskowitz
and Carl G. Lindbloom

The Illustrated Book
of Development
Definitions

About The Authors

HARVEY S. MOSKOWITZ, P.P., A.I.C.P., is a licensed professional planner and a former president of the New Jersey Board of Professional Planners. He has an undergraduate degree from Rutgers and an M.P.A. degree from New York University.

CARL G. LINDBLOOM, P.P., A.I.C.P., is planning consultant with offices in Princeton, New Jersey. He has an undergraduate degree in Architecture and a graduate degree in City Design from Miami University, Oxford, Ohio.

The Illustrated Book
of Development
Definitions

Harvey S. Moskowitz
Carl G. Lindbloom

CENTER
FOR URBAN
POLICY RESEARCH

RUTGERS UNIVERSITY • P.O. BOX 489
PISCATAWAY • NEW JERSEY • 08854

Published in the United States of America
by the Center for Urban Policy Research
Building 4051 — Kilmer Campus
New Brunswick, New Jersey 08903

Library of Congress Cataloging in Publication Data

Moskowitz, Harvey S.
The Illustrated Book of Development Definitions.
Includes index.
1. City planning—United States—Dictionaries. 2. Zoning—United
States—Dictionaries. 3. City planning and redevelopment law—
United States—Dictionaries. 4. Rural development—United States—
Dictionaries. I. Lindbloom, Carl G., joint author. II. Rutgers Univer-
sity, New Brunswick, N.J. Center for Urban Policy Research. III.
Title.

HT 167.M68   307.7'6'0321   80-21765
ISBN 0-88285-070-9 (pbk.)

Contents

List of Illustrations

A Note on the Use of the Book

Next to each definition in the text is a symbol indicating the types of ordinances in which the definition can usually be found. In looking up the definition of the word abandonment, for example, the user will find an accompanying symbol indicating that this definition is generally found in zoning ordinances. In addition, the Appendix contains an alphabetical listing of all the definitions with the same information checked in appropriate columns. After a particular ordinance is completed, the drafter can refer to the Appendix and read down the column for that particular ordinance and check to determine whether all appropriate definitions have been included.

Key to Symbols

▓	Zoning
▙	Subdivision
▛	Site Plan
▲	Environmental

Preface

This book differs from a number of other books of development definitions in three major respects: (a) it is illustrated; (b) most of the definitions are designed to be used directly in ordinances with little or no change; and (c) the more complex definitions are accompanied by commentaries and annotations which explain how the definition may be used in an ordinance and some legal background pertinent to the definition.

The primary purpose of including illustrations in this book is to aid in interpreting the definitions and to suggest they have a place in local ordinances as well. Unfortunately, illustrated definitions are rarely found in zoning and development ordinances. An occasional ordinance will show an angle-of-light diagram to establish the minimum dimension for interior courts or some similar complex and technical standard. But by far, ordinances prefer the "thousand words" rather than the "single picture." Regardless of the reasons, the omission of illustrations, even if only to highlight a definition or standard, is strange since the first zoning ordinance (New York City, 1916) was a series of three graphic overlays regulating height, use and bulk. Even today, the heart of a zoning ordinance is the district or zone map; and subdivision and site plan ordinances or elements are primarily concerned with design or graphic representations of what eventually will be three-dimensional products. Illustrations can greatly simplify how standards should be applied, particularly where the lot or parcel is irregularly shaped, or where there are a number of variables present, each of which might have an impact on how the ordinance might apply in a specific situation.

The concern that there might be a conflict between the written text and any diagram can be eliminated by specifying that in the event of such a conflict, the written text will have precedence.

The original intent of the authors was to prepare a book of definitions that could be used directly or with only slight modifications, in any zoning, subdivision or land development ordinance.[1] This presented certain obvious problems such as attempting to write a single definition which would be applicable equally to different kinds of municipalities in different states. In execution, however, this objective was not as difficult to achieve as it first appeared. One of the principles that the authors used and feel should be followed in writing any definition is not to include the standard which is being defined in the definition itself. Indeed, the standard itself may vary within the municipality by zoning district. Thus the definition for height, for example, can be constructed in such a manner that it can be applied universally while

---

[1]Throughout the book the terms zoning ordinance and land development ordinance are used synonymously. Actually, a land development ordinance is much broader in scope and application, covering all aspects of development including, in addition to zoning, subdivision, site plan, stormwater management, environmental impact and similar controls, standards and requirements. The reader is referred to the Appendix where each definition is assigned to an appropriate ordinance when individual ordinances are used rather than a comprehensive land development ordinance.

recognizing that the maximum or minimum standard will vary from municipality to municipality and even within municipalities. But how the height should be measured—from what point to what point—is equally applicable to New York City and East Alton, Illinois.

Occasionally, the attempt at universality and direct application broke down when the authors discovered two or even more equally adequate definitions covering the same word or term. For example, the definitions of RETAIL SERVICES, PERSONAL SERVICES, BUSINESS SERVICES and SOCIAL SERVICES overlap to a great extent but the reader may find one more appropriate than another for a particular municipality.

Finally, the use of commentaries and annotations suggest how the definition is designed to be used in development regulations and some legal discussion pertinent to the definition. While the commentaries are used primarily as a guide to the reader of this book, the authors suggest that commentaries can be useful in local ordinances as well. Very often the background and legislative intent can be included, a device often used in State legislation but rarely, if ever, in local codes. A brief note should be inserted at the beginning of the ordinance that the commentaries are only descriptive and explanatory and not part of the actual ordinance.

Acknowledgments

Most zoning or land development ordinance definitions are "borrowed" or "inherited" from other ordinances. Indeed, most ordinances are written in this way. If a planner is particularly astute, early on he or she will start collecting definitions; adding, discarding or modifying as the planner comes across new definitions or finds old ones not working. Many of the definitions in this book came about in this manner. But we do acknowledge other, particularly valuable contributions as follows:

1. The drafting committee of the New Jersey Municipal Land Use Law (Chapter 291, Laws of New Jersey, 1975) consisting of attorneys Harry Bernstein, Fred Stickel, III, Stewart Hutt, William Cox, Jim Jaeger, and planners Harry Maslow and Malcolm Kasler who labored long and hard in developing the final version of the Law. An important part of this law was the excellent set of definitions which covered almost all aspects of development.

2. The Standard Industrial Classification Manual, 1972 edition, Executive Office of the President, Office of Management & Budget. This book contains the best single source of definitions on all types of economic activity. We would like to see more planners use this source to allow definitions of various types of use activities to become standardized.

3. Acknowledgment also is given to those anonymous technicians in New Jersey government who helped write the New Jersey Casino Control Act (Chapter 110, Laws of 1977). From this document we secured the definitions related to casino gambling and casino operation.

4. The authors acknowledge the use of several excellent publications of the Urban Land Institute, particularly the Shopping Center Development Handbook, for definitions relating to shopping centers and other planned developments; the Atlantic City Land Use Ordinance for sign definitions; the N.J. Federation of Planning Official's bimonthly newsletter, *The Federation Planner,* with its annotation of many New Jersey planning and zoning cases; and the American Society of Planning Officials (now the American Planning Association) Planning Advisory Service research reports on zoning definitions.

5. The definitions relating to solar energy were taken from the U.S. Department of Housing and Development's new publication, *Protecting Solar Access for Residential Development, A Guidebook for Planning Officials.* That document and its companion piece, *Site Planning for Solar Access, A Guidebook for Residential Developers and Site Planners,* is recommended to all planners for practical suggestions for implementing what will no doubt be an increasingly important element in any future land development ordinances.

6. John Duryee, a member of the Planning Board of the Township of Cranford, N.J. and chairman of the land development ordinance subcommittee, focused an unusually critical eye

9

on many of the definitions and contributed extremely helpful suggestions to improve readability and application. William Cox, Esq., and Charles Agle, F.A.I.A., also suggested definitions which were incorporated in the book.

7.   Finally, much of the research for many of the definitions was undertaken by Megan Seel, a professional planner with a keen sense of organization, a practical knowledge of development ordinances, and the *sitzfleisch* needed to successfully complete the arduous task.

The authors particularly thank Linda Maschler who typed up what must have felt like 200 drafts of the book in her usual competent and expeditious manner. To all who assisted, whether directly or indirectly, we give our thanks. Naturally, the authors alone accept the responsibility for any mistakes that may appear in the book.

Introduction

How much lighter is light industry than heavy industry? Is there a difference between an advertising sign and business sign? Are the terms flood plain, flood hazard area and flood fringe area interchangeable?

The answers to these questions obviously depend on how we define our terms. And the purpose of this Illustrated Book of Development Definitions is to define some of the more common planning, development and environmental terms.

Purposes of Definitions

Webster defines "definition" as "a word or phrase expressing the essential nature of a person or thing or class of persons or of things, a statement of the meaning of a word or word group."[1] But definitions do more and when used in complex legal documents such as zoning ordinances or other development regulations, they have a threefold purpose:[2]

1. *They simplify the text*— By defining our terms, it is possible to combine into a single word long phrases, lists of words, or similar terms which, from a zoning or control point of view may be treated alike. For example, rather than repeat "application for site plan approval," "permission to build in a flood plain," "soil removal application" or "application for subdivision" in an ordinance regulating development, the phrase "application for development" can be defined to mean all of the preceding terms. Similarly, the term "manufacturing uses" is defined to mean:

> establishments engaged in the mechanical or chemical transformation of materials or substances into new products including the assembling of component parts, manufactured products, and the blending of materials such as lubricating oils, plastics, resins or liquors.

Think how long an ordinance would be if the definiens (the words used to describe the term to be defined) had to be repeated throughout the ordinance.

2. *Definitions precisely establish the meaning of a word or term which may be subject to differing interpretations*— The precise definition eliminates ambiguity and vagueness. It focuses on the essential elements of a word or phrase which clearly mark off and limit its

---

[1] *Webster's Third New International Dictionary,* (Springfield, Mass.: G. & C. Merriam Co., 1976).

[2] The reader is referred to Information Report No. 72, *Planning Definitions,* Planning Advisory Service, American Society of Planning Officials, (now American Planning Association), March 1955, for a more detailed discussion on the theory of zoning definitions. The material on the objectives of definitions is adopted from that excellent publication.

11

application or interpretation except as the writer of the ordinance intended.

For example, a zone may permit light industrial uses. Everyone knows what light industry is—right? Industry is—well, work. Or is it manufacturing? Is warehousing included? Webster has five definitions of industry and the authoritative Standard Industrial Classification Manual lists retailing, finance, and real estate under the broad definition of industry. So it is not quite that apparent, and even experts could impart different meanings to the word.

If we consider defining *industry* difficult, we must acknowledge the equally difficult problem of defining *light* in conjunction with industry. Does light refer to the end product? The raw material? The machines used in the process? Or does it refer to something else completely?

By precisely defining light industry in an ordinance, we eliminate the vagueness and ambiguity which at best, results in confusion and at worst, ends up in costly lawsuits and delays.

3. *Definitions translate technical terms into usable and understandable terminology*—
Definitions enable us to convert sometimes abstract technical terms into meaningful standards to control and guide development.

For example, the term *light* as used in *light* industry may be defined in terms of a number of variables such as trip generation, bulk controls, and nuisance characteristics.[3] Each of these terms requires further definition to make the original "light industry" term meaningful and enforceable.

Thus, one nuisance characteristic may be smoke emission, and the defined characteristic of light industry in terms of smoke emission is that the smoke density cannot exceed #1 on the Ringelmann Chart, the standard measure of smoke density. Another nuisance characteristic is noise, and light industry can be further defined as industry where the noise level measured at the lot line does not exceed certain decibels in a particular frequency range.

What Definitions are Not

Given that definitions simplify, clarify, and translate, it might be well to point out what definitions should not be. The most important limitation is that the definition should not contain the control elements or standards which regulate the intensity or bulk of the defined uses. For example, most ordinances attempt to define home occupations in terms of the standards under which the home occupation can be established. These standards usually include the percentage of floor area that can be occupied, limitations on nonresident employees, parking requirements, etc.

These controls belong in the body of the ordinance and in fact may vary depending on the zone in which the home occupation is permitted. To locate the standards in the definition precludes this flexibility.

Another example of misplaced standards is often found with our previously cited *light industry*. The definition of light industry should read:

LIGHT INDUSTRY— Industrial uses which meet the performance standards, bulk controls and other requirements established in this ordinance.

The ordinance would then spell out the performance standards and bulk controls to which light industry must conform. In fact, as illustrated below, the controls on medium and heavy

---

[3]It is not defined in terms of the end product, raw material or the size of machines used in the process. See comment under "light industry" in the text.

industry also could be included and the definition of medium and heavy industry need not be substantially different than light industry.[4]

A typical control chart might read as follows:

Control Elements	Light Industry	Medium Industry	Heavy Industry
Minimum lot size	no minimum	5 acres	10 acres
Maximum lot size	5 acres	10 acres	no limit
Maximum FAR	.5	1.0	2.0
Max. Building Height	2 stories/30'	4 stories/60'	6 stories/80'
Max. # of vehicle trips per peak hour	100	300	no limit
Maximum noise level	70 dBA	75 dBA	82 dBA
Max. smoke density on Ringlemann Chart	#1	#1	#2
Vibration	none permitted beyond bldg. wall	none permitted beyond lot line	none permitted beyond zone line
Air pollution	50% of max. allowed by State law	75% of max. allowed by State law	as permitted by State law

Note: The list of control elements noted above is not complete and standards suggested are for illustration purposes only. The chart does illustrate the point—the definition is four lines and simple; the standard in the ordinance may be long and detailed.

Definitions also should not run counter to the generally accepted meaning of words and phrases. As someone pointed out, "If it quacks like a duck, walks like a duck, etc." Very often this problem manifests itself in a negative manner. A zoning ordinance may establish a retail commercial zone and then exclude an obvious retail use because of local pressures, fear of competition, or real or perceived impacts. The point is that the generally accepted meaning of words and phrases should not be radically altered in an ordinance.

By the same token, however, common words and phrases often take on a specific meaning in a technical field which may differ substantially from the generally accepted or public definition. Some examples are cellar, basement, home occupation, etc. The courts also may restrict or expand commonly accepted definitions. The best illustration is the word "family" which recent State Court decisions have expanded to include an unlimited number of non-related individuals.

Real vs. Nominal Definitions

The previously cited Planning Advisory Service Report No. 72, *Planning Definitions,* had an excellent discussion on real and nominal definitions. It defined a nominal definition as ". . . one adopted more or less arbitrarily but which need not be a true description of the object denoted." (See p. 8.) A real definition is an attempt to precisely describe the object, use or term.

Real definitions are preferred but very often this goal becomes difficult to achieve. For example, the term density may be defined as the number of dwelling units per acre of land. For control or regulation purposes, it requires a further clarification to determine whether it is a net figure (excluding certain classes or types of land) or a gross figure (inclusive of the entire area

---

[4]A municipality might want to allow outdoor storage in heavy industrial districts and amend the light industry definition accordingly.

within the described boundaries). Thus, the real definition of density requires two (or even more) nominal definitions to be utilized effectively in the ordinance.

To avoid the problem of whether a definition is real or nominal, most zoning or development ordinances usually preface the definition section with a phrase similar to the following:

Unless the context clearly indicates a different meaning, for the purposes of this ordinance, the following words and terms shall be defined as follows.

Some General Observations About Definitions in Development Ordinances

1. *Don't define it if it is not used in the ordinance—* There are two schools of thought on whether to include a word or phrase which is not subsequently included in the ordinance. For example, in a rural farming municipality, should the term high-rise apartment be defined? Conversely, in a built-up urban area, should the term farm be defined?

Many drafters feel that if there is a possibility that the phrase will be used in the future, it should be included. The authors feel differently. If it is not used it should not be defined. The reason is that it may confuse the intent of the framers. If high-rise apartments are not permitted, then there is no reason to include it anywhere in the ordinance.[5] In addition, where there may be a question as to the intent of whether or not a particular use is allowed in a zone, the fact that it is defined gives credence to the position that the intent was to allow the use.

2. *Use federal, state or county definitions if available—* More and more categories of land use are no longer under local control, or require federal, state or county licenses or approval even where the municipality exercises locational control. In order to avoid conflicts, the local definition should agree with the "higher" definition. It also more clearly defines the intent of the framers in allowing a specific type of use or activity in a zone. For example, all states license schools and most license various categories of health care facilities. If the local intent is to permit elementary schools in residential neighborhoods, then the definition can be "any school licensed by the State and which meets the State requirements for elementary education." This eliminates business schools, vocational schools, etc.

County requirements and definitions relating to roads and streets are particularly appropriate for inclusion in local development codes.

3. *Use nationally accepted definitions if available—* The best single source of use definitions is the *Standard Industrial Classification Manual.*[6] The *SICM* groups all land use activities in a series of categories from very broad activity classes (residential, manufacturing, trade, services, etc.) to very specific and detailed land use categories. The most detailed category (defined as the four-digit category) contains 772 land use activities. The three-digit category contains 294 classes, two-digit 67 activities, and the broadest category, 9 major activities.

Thus, major group 82, Educational Services, is part of Division I, SERVICES. The three-digit group includes #821, Elementary and Secondary Schools; #822, Colleges, Universities, Professional Schools, and Junior Colleges; #823, Libraries and Information Centers; etc. A further breakdown into specific types of activities takes place at the four-digit

---

[5]The one exception may be in an ordinance which lists prohibited uses. Then the definition of the prohibited use becomes important. Prohibitive use ordinances generally are being replaced by permissive ordinances since, among other reasons, no ordinance could possibly list all the excluded uses.

[6]*Standard Industrial Classification Manual,* Statistical Policy Division, Executive Office of the President, Office of Management & Budget (Washington, D.C.: Government Printing Office, 1972).

level. However, for purposes of defining land use activities, the three-digit level appears adequate. Examples of each type of activity are included as well as comprehensive definitions in the two- and four-digit levels.

Summary

To summarize, and using in part the Planning Advisory Service's previously quoted report:

1. The term being defined (a) must be exactly equivalent to the definition; (b) should not appear in the definition; (c) cannot be defined by a synonym; and (d) should not be defined by other indefinite or ambiguous terms.

2. Definitions phrased in positive terms are preferable to definitions in negative terms.

3. Definitions should not include the standards, measurements or other control regulations.

4. Anything not specifically *included* in a definition is automatically *excluded*.

5. A defined term can have none other but the defined meaning throughout the entire ordinance.

6. If a group of objects is being divided into two or more groups by definitions, be sure that *all* members of the group are *included* in one or the other of the groups.

7. Use particular care in the grammatical construction of definitions.

8. Do not define terms that are not used in the ordinance.

9. Check definitions in related local ordinances and use county, state or federal regulations where appropriate.

10. Use nationally known standard definitions when available.

The Illustrated Book
of Development
Definitions

Development Definitions

A

ABANDONMENT

The relinquishment of property, or a cessation of the use of the property, by the owner with the intention neither of transferring rights to the property to another owner nor of resuming the use of the property.

Comment: In zoning, abandonment of a nonconforming use requires (a) a discontinuance of the use and, (b) an intent to abandon. (*Shack* v. *Trumble, 28 N.J. 40, 1958; Marino* v. *Mayor and Council of Norwood, 77 N.J. Super 587, L.D. 1963*). Since intent is often difficult to prove, many zoning ordinances sidestep the issue by stating that a nonconforming use not exercised for a period of time (one year, for example) may not be resumed.

ABATEMENT

The method of reducing the degree and intensity of pollution.

ABSORPTION

The penetration of one substance into or through another.

ABUT

To physically touch or border upon; or to share a common property line. *See* ADJOINING LOT or LAND and CONTIGUOUS.

ACCELERATION LANE

An added roadway lane which permits integration and merging of slower moving vehicles into the main vehicular stream. *See Figure 1.*

19

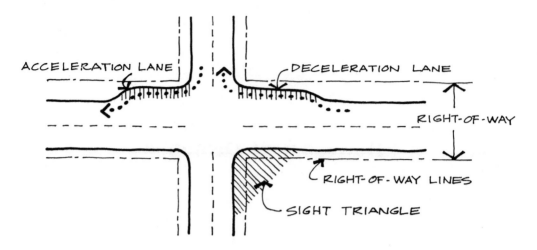

Figure 1

 **ACCESS**

A way or means of approach to provide physical entrance to a property.

 ACCESS ROAD

See STREET, LOCAL.

ACCESSORY STRUCTURE

A structure detached from a principal building on the same lot and customarily incidental and subordinate to the principal building or use. *See Figure 22.*

Comment: Often it is desirable to place limits on the number and size of accessory structures, particularly in residential areas.

ACCESSORY USE

A use of land or of a building or portion thereof customarily incidental and subordinate to the principal use of the land or building and located on the same lot with such principal use.

ACCLIMATIZATION

The physiological and behavioral adjustments of an organism over time to a marked change in the environment.

ACCRETION

The creation of land by the recession of a lake or stream or by the gradual deposit of solid material by water.

ACRE

A measure of land area containing 43,560 square feet.

Comment: Many ordinances use a "builder's acre" of 40,000 square feet.

20

◭ ACRE-FOOT

The volume of water one foot deep covering an acre of land.

Comment: Used in defining storage capacity.

◭ ACTIVATED CARBON

A highly absorbant form of carbon used to remove odors and toxic substances from gaseous emissions.

◭ ACTIVATED SLUDGE PROCESS

The process of using biologically active sewage sludge to hasten the breakdown of organic matter in raw sewage during secondary waste treatment.

▛◭ ADAPTATION

A change in structure or habit of an organism that produces better adjustment to the environment.

▛◭ ADAPTIVE REUSE

The development of a new use for an older building or for a building originally designed for a special or specific purpose.

Comment: Adaptive reuse is particularly useful as a technique for preserving older buildings of historic or architectural significance, but also applies to the conversion of gas stations, school buildings and other special use buildings no longer needed for their original purpose.

▛ ADDITION

A structure added to the original structure at some time after the completion of the original.

Comment: "At some time after" is usually defined as after the certificate of occupancy has been issued for the original structure.

▛◭ ADJACENT LAND

See ADJOINING LOT or LAND.

▛◭ ADJOINING LOT OR LAND

A lot or parcel of land which shares all or part of a common lot line with another lot or parcel of land. *See* ABUT and CONTIGUOUS.

▛◭ ADMINISTRATIVE OFFICE

An establishment primarily engaged in management and general administrative functions such as executive, personnel, finance, and sales activities performed centrally for other establishments of the same company.

▛◭ ADMINISTRATIVE OFFICER

The governmental officer charged with administering land development regulations.

21

ADULT BOOK STORE   A retail establishment selling publications and other material of a sexual nature.

ADVANCED WASTE TREATMENT   Waste water treatment beyond the secondary or biological stage that includes removal of nutrients such as phosphates and nitrogen and a high percentage of suspended solids.

Comment: Advanced waste treatment, known as tertiary treatment, is the "polishing stage" of waste water treatment and produces a high quality effluent.

ADVERSE POSSESSION   The right of an occupant to acquire title to a property after having continuously and openly used and maintained a property over a statutory period of time without protest from the owner of record.

ADVERTISING DISPLAY   *See* SIGN.

AERATION   The process of being supplied or impregnated with air.

Comment: Aeration is used in waste water treatment to foster biological and chemical purification.

AERIAL MAP   A map created from a process involving the taking of photographs from the air.

AEROBIC   Life or processes that can occur only in the presence of oxygen.

AEROSOL   A suspension of liquid or solid particles in the air.

AESTHETIC   The perception of artistic elements, or elements in the natural or man-made environment which are pleasing to the eye.

AESTHETIC ZONING   Regulations designed to preserve or improve building or site development so as to be more pleasing to the eye.

Comment: What constitutes "more pleasing" is difficult to define. But planning also has had an aesthetic orientation; the origins of city planning were in the "city beautiful" movement beginning with the Columbia Exposition in 1893. While early court decisions failed to sustain aesthetics solely as a basis for the exercise of the

22

police power, the shift in recent cases suggest a more pragmatic approach. In *Berman* v. *Parker,* (348 U.S. 26, 1954), the Court recognized the right of the legislature to determine that beauty is a valid objective of police power authority.

Ordinances that purport to regulate aesthetics, however, often have problems with standards upon which to judge the "aesthetics" of an application. Unless an area is an official historic area, or other special design district, architectural design probably remains outside the scope of such regulations. The bulk of aesthetic regulations focus on sign control, fence regulations, landscaping and buffering. *See* ARCHITECTURAL CONTROL.

AFTERBURNER

An air pollution abatement device that removes undesirable organic gases through incineration.

AGRARIAN

Relating to land; particularly agriculture.

AGRICULTURAL MARKET

Any fixed or mobile retail food establishment which is engaged primarily in the sale of raw agricultural products, but may include as accessory to the principal use, the sale of factory-sealed or prepackaged food products that normally do not require refrigeration. *See* FARM STAND.

AGRICULTURAL POLLUTION

The liquid and solid wastes from all types of farming, including runoff from pesticides, fertilizers and feedlots; erosion and dust from plowing, animal manure and carcasses, and crop residue and debris.

AGRICULTURAL SERVICES

Establishments primarily engaged in supplying soil preparation services, crop services, landscaping, horticultural services, veterinary and other animal services and farm labor and management services.

AGRICULTURE

The production, keeping or maintenance, for sale, lease or personal use, of plants and animals useful to man, including but not limited to: forages and sod crops; grains and seed crops; dairy animals and dairy products, poultry and poultry products; livestock, including beef cattle, sheep, swine, horses, ponies, mules, or goats, or any mutations or hybrids thereof, including the breeding and grazing of any or all of such animals; bees and apiary products; fur animals; trees and forest products; fruits of all kinds, including grapes, nuts and berries; vege-

23

tables; nursery, floral, ornamental and greenhouse products; or lands devoted to a soil conservation or forestry management program. *See* HORTICULTURE.

Comment: The definition is based on the definition contained in the N.J. Farmland Assessment Act (C.48, L. 1964, N.J.S.A. 54:4–23.1 *et seq.*) and is broadly defined. It includes intensive agricultural activities such as feedlot operations, chicken farms and agribusiness activities, some of which may not be appropriate in all areas.

AIR PARK

A complex of uses such as offices, stores, hotels, and manufacturers that adjoin or are part of an airport and requiring or desiring close access thereto.

AIR POLLUTION

The presence of contaminants in the air in concentrations that prevent the normal dispensive ability of the air and that interfere directly or indirectly with man's health, safety or comfort or with the full use and enjoyment of his property.

AIR POLLUTION EPISODE

The occurrence of abnormally high concentrations of air pollutants usually due to low winds and temperature inversion which may be accompanied by increases in illness and death. *See* INVERSION.

AIR QUALITY CONTROL REGION

An area designated by the Federal government where two or more communities—either in the same or different states—share a common air pollution problem.

AIR QUALITY CRITERIA

The levels of pollution and length of exposure at which adverse effects on health and welfare occur.

AIR QUALITY STANDARDS

The prescribed level of pollutants in the outside air that cannot be exceeded legally during a specified time in a specified geographical area.

AIR RIGHTS

The right to use space above ground level.

Comment: Air rights are usually purchased or leased from the property owner and are often over highways and railroads. New York City's historic preservation program permits the purchase of air rights over historic structures to be used to increase the height and/or intensity of development on nonhistoric properties.

AIR TRANSPORTATION — Establishments engaged in domestic and foreign transportation by air including airports, flying fields, as well as terminal services.

AIRPORT — A place where aircraft can land and take off, usually equipped with hangers, facilities for refueling and repair and various accommodations for passengers.

AISLE — The travelled way by which cars enter and depart parking spaces. *See Figure 2.*

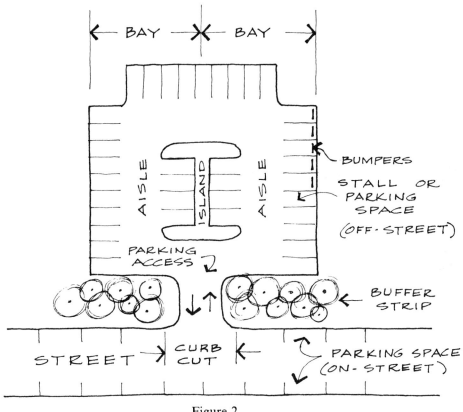

Figure 2

ALLEY — A service way providing a secondary means of public access to abutting property and not intended for general traffic circulation.

ALLUVION — That increase of land area on a shore or bank of a stream or sea, by the force of the water, as by a current or by waves, which is so gradual that it is impossible to determine how much is added at each moment of time.

25

 **ALTERATION**

Any change or rearrangement in the supporting members of an existing building, such as bearing walls, columns, beams, girders or interior partitions, as well as any change in doors or windows, or any enlargement to or diminution of a building or structure, whether horizontally or vertically, or the moving of a building or structure from one location to another.

Comment: The definition of alteration is important because most ordinances do not permit any alteration to a nonconforming structure or use. This definition excludes normal repairs and maintenance, such as painting, but includes more substantial changes. *See* STRUCTURAL ALTERATION.

AMBIENT AIR

Any unconfined portion of the atmosphere; the outside air.

AMBIENT AIR STANDARD

A maximum permissible air pollution standard.

AMENITY

A natural or man-made feature which enhances or makes more attractive or satisfying a particular property.

AMORTIZATION

A method of eliminating nonconforming uses by requiring the termination of the nonconforming use after a specified period of time.

Comment: The legality of requiring the amortization of nonconforming uses still remains unclear. Hagmann (*Urban Planning and Land Development Control Laws,* Hornbook Series, West Publishing Company, p. 159) notes that, "Great public need . . . (for) . . . uses externalizing harm, is used to justify termination of nonconforming uses without compensation." The leading case on the subject is *City of Los Angeles* v. *Gage* (127 Cal. App. 2d 442, 274 P.2d 34,1954). The most likely candidates for amortization are signs because of their relatively low cost and junkyards which, in addition to not having a great deal of capital investment, are highly visible nuisances.

AMUSEMENT AND RECREATION SERVICES

Establishments engaged in providing amusement or entertainment for a fee or admission charge and include such activities as dance halls; studios; theatrical producers; bands, orchestras, and other musical entertainment; bowling alleys and billiard and pool establish-

26

ments; commercial sports such as arenas, rings, race-tracks, public golf courses and coin-operated devices; amusement parks; membership sports and recreation clubs; amusement and bathing beaches; swimming pools; riding academies; carnival operations; expositions; game parlors and horse shows.

Comment: The above definition is a broad one covering all types of amusement and recreational facilities. It is a suitable one for a resort area but more limited definitions are listed below.

AMUSEMENT FACILITY

An outdoor area or structure, open to the public, which contains coin operated games, and similar entertainment and amusement devices. *See* RECREATION FACILITY.

AMUSEMENT PARK

An outdoor facility, which may include structures and buildings, where there are various devices for entertainment, including rides, booths for the conduct of games or sale of items, and buildings for shows and entertainment.

ANCHOR STORE

See ANCHOR TENANT and MAGNET STORE.

ANCHOR TENANT

The major store or stores within a shopping center.

Comment: The anchor tenant is a full-line department store of at least 100,000 square feet, is the most important tenant in a shopping center and the one that generates the customer traffic. Super-regional centers (750,000 square feet or more) may have three or more anchor stores.

ANEROBIC

Refers to life or processes that occur in the absence of oxygen.

ANIMAL HOSPITAL

A place where animals or pets are given medical or surgical treatment and the boarding of animals is limited to short-term care incidental to the hospital use.

ANIMAL KENNEL

Any structure or premises in which animals are kept, boarded, bred or trained for commercial gain. *See* KENNEL.

ANIMATED SIGN

See SIGN.

ANNEXATION

The incorporation of a land area into an existing community with a resulting change in the boundaries of that community.

27

◩ ANTI-DEGRADATION CLAUSE   A provision in air quality and water quality laws that prohibits deterioration of air or water quality in areas where the pollution levels are presently below those allowed.

◩ ▢ APARTMENT, GARDEN   *See* DWELLING, GARDEN APARTMENT.

◩ ▢ APARTMENT, HIGH-RISE   *See* DWELLING, HIGH-RISE.

◩ ▢ APARTMENT HOUSE   A structure containing three or more apartment units. *See* DWELLING, MULTIFAMILY.

◩ ▢ APARTMENT, MID-RISE   *See* DWELLING, MID-RISE.

◩ ▢ APARTMENT UNIT   One or more rooms with private bath and kitchen facilities comprising an independent self-contained dwelling unit in a building containing more than two dwelling units.

◩ ▢ APARTMENT UNIT, EFFICIENCY   *See* DWELLING UNIT, EFFICIENCY.

◩▸▢◮ APPLICANT   A person submitting an application for development.

◩▸▢◮ APPLICATION FOR DEVELOPMENT   The application form and all accompanying documents and exhibits required of an applicant by an approving authority for development review purposes.

◩ APPRAISAL   An estimate or opinion of the value of real or personal property or an interest or estate in that property as determined by a qualified appraiser.

◩▸▢◮ APPROVED PLAN   A plan which has been granted final approval by the appropriate approving authority.

◩▸▢◮ APPROVING AUTHORITY   The agency, board, group or other legally designated individual or authority which has been charged with review and approval of plans and applications.

◮ AQUACULTURE PROJECT   A controlled discharge of pollutants to enhance growth or propagation of harvestable freshwater, estuarine, or marine life plant or animal species.

	AQUARIUM	A building where collections of live water plants and animals are exhibited.
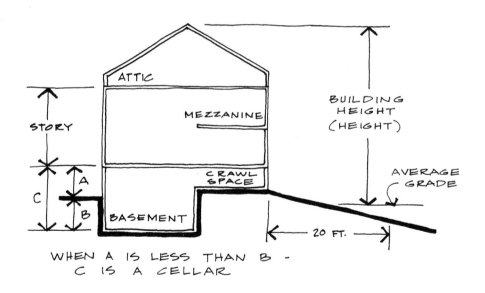	**AQUATIC PLANTS**	Plants that grow in water either floating on the surface, growing up from the bottom of the body of water or growing under the surface of the water.
	AQUIFER	An underground bed or stratum of earth, gravel or porous stone that contains water. *See Figure 31.*
	AQUIFER RECHARGE AREA	The exposed ground level portion of the aquifer.
	ARCADE	A continuous passageway parallel to and open to a street, open space, or building, usually covered by a canopy or permanent roofing, and accessible and open to the public. *See Figure 13.*
	ARCHAEOLOGICAL SITE	Land or water areas which show evidence or artifacts of human, plant or animal activity, usually dating from periods of which only vestiges remain.

Figure 3

29

 **ARCHITECTURAL CONTROL**

Public regulation of the design of private buildings to develop, preserve or enhance the attractiveness or character of a particular area or individual buildings.

Comment: Aesthetic reasons are the main purpose architectural controls are imposed. The leading case on the subject is State ex rel. *Saveland Park Holding Corp.* v. *Wieland* (269 Wis. 202, 69 N.W. 2d 217, 1955) which upheld denial of a building permit for a building at variance with its neighbor. While aesthetics was cited as a major reason for upholding the denial, the issue of protecting property values was also cited. In all ordinances calling for architectural controls, the standards upon which to judge a particular building must be precise and carefully drawn to avoid charges of vagueness and improper delegation of authority. *See* Aesthetic Zoning.

 **AREA SCALE**

A graphic display of the relationship between areas on a map and actual areas. *See* Scale. *See Figure 24.*

 **AREA SOURCE**

In air pollution, any small individual fuel combustion source, including any transportation source. *See* Point Source.

Comment: This is a general definition; area source is usually specifically set forth and precisely defined in appropriate federal statutes.

ARTERIAL STREET

See Street, Major Arterial.

ARTESIAN AQUIFER

An aquifer in which water is confined under pressure between layers of impermeable material.

ARTIFICIAL RECHARGE

Adding water to an aquifer by artificial means such as specially designed wells, ditches, or through other man-made methods.

ARTS CENTER

A structure or complex of structures for housing the visual and/or performing arts.

A-SCALE SOUND LEVEL

The measurement of sound approximating the auditory sensitivity of the human ear and used to measure the relative noisiness or annoyance of common sounds.

ASSEMBLAGE

The merger of separate properties into a single tract of land. *See* Consolidation.

ASSESSED VALUATION

The value at which property is appraised for tax purposes.

Comment: It is often expressed as a percentage of the value which has been placed upon the property for tax purposes.

 ASSESSMENT RATIO

The relation between the assessed value of a property and true market value.

Comment: For a number of reasons the assessed value of property may not reflect market value. In some states, communities are permitted to assess at a percentage of true market value. In addition, in jurisdictions that do not reassess or revalue frequently, the discrepancy between assessed valuation and true market value may increase significantly. In order to equalize all properties within a given taxing jurisdiction, some regional or state agency will assign an equalization ratio to a community's property. The planner must consider this equalization ratio in undertaking any cost benefit analysis. For example, an improvement with a market value of $500,000, because of an equalization ratio of 80%, may be only assessed at $400,000.

ASSIMILATION

Conversion or incorporation of absorbed nutrients into protoplasm; the ability of a body of water to purify itself of organic pollution.

ATMOSPHERE

The layer of air surrounding the earth. *See Figure 31.*

ATTACHED DWELLING UNIT

See DWELLING, ATTACHED.

ATTENTION GETTING DEVICE

A device designed or intended to attract by noise, sudden intermittent or rhythmic movement, physical change or lighting change, such as banners, flags, streamers, balloons, propellers, whirligigs, search lights and flashing lights.

ATTIC

That part of a building which is immediately below and wholly or partly within the roof framing. *See* STORY, HALF. *See Figure 3.*

AUDIOMETER

An instrument for measuring hearing sensitivity.

31

▣	**AUTOMATIC CAR WASH**	A structure containing facilities for washing automobiles using a chain conveyor or other method of moving the cars along, and automatic or semiautomatic application of cleaner, brushes, rinse water and heat for drying.
▣	**AUTOMOBILE**	A self-propelled free moving vehicle, with four or more wheels, primarily for conveyance on a street or roadway.
▣	**AUTOMOBILE REPAIR**	*See* GARAGE, REPAIR.
▣	**AUTOMOBILE SALES**	The use of any building, land area or other premise for the display and sale of new or used automobiles, panel trucks or vans, trailers, or recreation vehicles and including any warranty repair work and other repair service conducted as an accessory use.
▣	**AUTOMOBILE SERVICE STATION**	Any building, land area or other premises, or portion thereof, used or intended to be used for the retail dispensing or sales of vehicular fuels; and including as an accessory use the sale and installation of lubricants, tires, batteries and similar accessories.
▣	**AUTOMOBILE WASH**	Any building or premises or portions thereof used for washing automobiles.
▣	**AUTOMOBILE WRECKING YARD**	*See* JUNKYARD.
▣	**AUTOMOTIVE REPAIR SERVICES AND GARAGES**	Establishments primarily engaged in furnishing automotive repair, rental, leasing and parking services to the general public.

Comment: This general category includes all of the major components of the automotive industry (except the dispensing of gas and oil directly into the vehicles) including parking lots and structures, all types of repairs, car washes and rental and leasing activities.

⬛	**AUTOTROPHIC**	Self-nourishing; denoting those organisms capable of constructing organic matter from inorganic substances.
▣ ▮	**AVIATION EASEMENT**	*See* EASEMENT, AVIATION.
⬛	**AVULSION**	A sudden and perceptible loss or addition to land by the action of water or otherwise.

32

AWNING	A roof-like cover that is temporary in nature and that projects from the wall of a building for the purpose of shielding a doorway or window from the elements. *See Figure 26.*

Comment: The key phrase is that awnings are *temporary* in nature. Once they become permanent, then all setbacks should be measured from the end of the awning. Otherwise, as temporary awnings, they can project into required yards.

B

BACK-TO-BACK LOTS	Separate land parcels which have at least half of each rear lot line coterminous.
BACKFILL	Material used to refill a ditch or other excavation, or the process of doing so.
BACKGROUND LEVEL	Amounts of pollutants present in the ambient air due to natural sources.
BACKGROUND RADIATION	Normal radiation present in the lower atmosphere from cosmic rays and from earth sources.
BACTERIA	Single-celled microorganisms that lack chlorophyll.
BAFFLE	Any deflector device used to change the direction or the flow of water, sewage, products or combustion such as fly ash or coarse particulate matter, or of sound waves.
BALING	A means of reducing the volume of solid waste by compaction.
BALLISTIC SEPARATOR	A machine that separates inorganic from organic matter in a compositing process.
BAR	A structure or part of a structure used primarily for the sale or dispensing of liquor by the drink.

Comment: In developing zoning regulations to regulate bars, a distinction is often made between bars that have live entertainment and those that do not. Those with live entertainment require considerably more parking and additional setbacks because of noise. Many bars also possess licenses which permit them to sell bottled goods. This is usually accessory to the principal use of dispensing liquor by the drink.

BAR SCREEN

In waste water treatment, a device that removes large floating and suspended solids.

BARRIER

A device that prevents traffic from crossing into the path of traffic flowing in an opposite direction. *See* MEDIAN ISLAND.

BARRIER ISLAND

Land area, separated on all sides by water, usually elongated and formed by the action of the sea on land, that protects the mainland from sea action.

BASE FLOOD ELEVATION

The highest elevation, expressed in feet above sea level, of the level of flood waters occurring in the regulatory base flood.

Comment: The base flood elevation represents the worst flooding experience in a community or an area. Regulation promulgated by various regulatory agencies such as HUD permit construction in certain flood-prone areas provided that such new construction is elevated or raised a given dimension from the base flood elevation and that other flood damage prevention measures are taken.

BASE MAP

A map having sufficient points of reference, such as state, county or municipal boundary lines, streets, easements, and other selected physical features to allow the plotting of other data.

BASEMENT

A space having one-half or more of its floor-to-ceiling height above the average level of the adjoining ground and with a floor-to-ceiling height of not less than 6½ feet. *See Figure 3.*

Comment: Municipalities often run into difficulty with respect to the regulation of basements. Generally speaking, if a basement is used only for heating, mechanical and similar equipment, it is not counted either as a story or in computing the intensity of development such as floor area ratio, etc. If it is used for storage purposes pertaining to the principal use, for dwelling unit pur-

34

poses, or for office space or a similar function, it is counted both as a story and included in whatever standards are used to control the intensity of development.

 **BASIN**

An area drained by the main stream and tributaries of a large river.

 **BEACH**

A nearly level stretch of pebbles and/or sand beside a sea or lake which may be man-made or created by the action of the water. *See* INTERTIDAL AREA.

 BEDROCK

In-place geologic formations which cannot be removed with conventional excavating equipment, or which, upon excavation, includes more than 60% formation fragments (by weight) that are retained in a one-quarter-inch mesh screen.

Comment: The above definition is from the New Jersey Department of Environmental Protection's Standards for the Construction of Individual Subsurface Sewage Disposal Systems.

 **BEDROOM**

A private room planned and intended for sleeping, separable from other rooms by a door, and accessible to a bathroom without crossing another bedroom or living room.

 **BELTWAY**

A highway, usually of limited access, around an area of high traffic congestion or urban development. *See Figure 32.*

 **BERM**

A mound of earth, or the act of pushing earth into a mound. *See Figure 23.*

Comment: Berms are usually 2 to 6 feet high and are used to shield and buffer uses such as parking areas. They also serve to control the direction of water flow and act as dams.

BIKEWAY

A pathway, often paved and separated from streets and sidewalks, designed to be used by bikers. *See Figure 23.*

Comment: The bikeway has now become accepted as a necessary part of the circulation system. The Federal Department of Transportation and various state highway departments have set forth specific standards for various classifications of bikeways.

BILLBOARD   *See* SIGN, BILLBOARD.

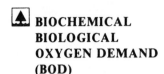 **BIOCHEMICAL BIOLOGICAL OXYGEN DEMAND (BOD)**

A measure of the amount of oxygen consumed in the biological processes that break down organic matter in water.

Comment: Large amounts of organic waste use up large amounts of dissolved oxygen, thus the greater the degree of pollution, the higher the BOD.

BIODEGRADABLE

Capable of being decomposed by the action of micro-organisms.

BIOLOGICAL CONTROL

A method of controlling pests by means of introduced or naturally occurring predatory organisms, sterilization or the use of inhibiting hormones, or similar methods, rather than by mechanical or chemical means.

BIOLOGICAL OXIDATION

The process by which bacterial and other microorganisms feed on complex organic materials and decompose them. Also known as biochemical oxidation.

Comment: Self-purification of waterways and activated sludge and trickling filter waste water treatment processes depend on the principle of biological oxidation.

BIOMONITORING

The use of living organisms to test the suitability of effluent for discharge into receiving waters and to test the quality of such waters downstream from a discharge.

BIOSPHERE

The portion of the earth and its atmosphere capable of supporting life.

BIOSTABILIZER

A machine used to convert solid waste into compost by grinding and aeration.

BIOTA

All the species of plants and animals occurring within a certain area.

BLENDING

The joining of two or more materials which combine chemically to form a new product differing chemically from either of the original materials.

Comment: The process of blending usually involves gases, liquids or chemicals, but may involve solids which are physically combined in a manner in which the individual components lose their original identities.

36

| | BLIGHTED AREA | An area characterized by deteriorating and/or abandoned buildings, inadequate or missing public or community services, vacant land with debris, litter, lack of sanitation facilities, trash and junk accumulation, and impacted by adverse environmental nuisances such as noise, heavy traffic, and odors.

Comment: An alternate definition could refer to appropriate state enabling legislation. Or, the zoning definition could define a blighted area in the following comprehensive manner:

A blighted area has specific legal terminology in the application of federal and state funding. Under the Housing Act of 1949 as amended, and various state acts, an area which meets the definition contained in these acts can be acquired by public agencies and resold to private developers for the purpose of redevelopment and renewal.

 BLOCK

A unit of land bounded by streets or by a combination of streets and public land, railroad rights-of-way, waterways or any other barrier to the continuity to development. *See Figure 18.*

BLOCK STATISTICS

United States census information tabulated on a block basis.

BLOOM

A proliferation of living algae and/or other aquatic plants on the surface of lakes or ponds.

BOARD OF ADJUSTMENT

An officially constituted body whose principal duties are to grant variances from the strict application of the zoning ordinance.

Comment: The work and name of the board of adjustment varies by state. In New Jersey, for example, appeals from zoning decisions of the zoning officer are taken to the board of adjustment. The board of adjustment also interprets the zoning ordinance and the zoning map, grants variances from the bulk and dimension requirements of the ordinance, and unlike many other states, can grant a variance for a use not specifically permitted in the zone. In some states, boards of adjustment are called boards of standards and appeals.

BOARDER

An individual other than a member of the family occupying the dwelling unit or a part thereof who, for a consideration, is furnished sleeping accommodations and may be furnished meals or other services as part of the consideration.

Comment: Many older zoning ordinances distinguished between roomers or boarders, the latter usually being a person who received meals as part of the consideration. More modern ordinances do not make the distinction. Older ordinances also make a distinction between temporary and permanent boarders which is not a particularly meaningful difference.

BOARDING HOME FOR SHELTERED CARE

A profit or nonprofit boarding home, rest home, or other home for the sheltered care of adult persons which, in addition to providing food and shelter to four or more persons unrelated to the proprietor, also provides any personal care or service beyond food, shelter and laundry.

Comment: The sheltered care facility serves as a substitute for the residents' own homes, furnishing facilities and comforts normally found in a home but providing in addition such service, equipment, and safety features as are required for safe and adequate care of residents at all times. Such services may include: (1) supervision and assistance in dressing, bathing, and in the maintenance of good personal hygiene; (2) care in emergencies or during temporary illness, usually for periods of one week or less; (3) supervision in the taking of medications; and (4) other services conducive to the residents' welfare. For purposes of zoning and districting, the boarding home for sheltered care may include half-way houses, homes for battered spouses and children, and homes designed to provide a transition from long-term institutional care to normal activities. Zoning regulations might include these facilities as conditional uses and include standards or maximum occupancy based on the square footage of the house (for example, 150 square feet of bedroom space per occupant), adequate parking and, if in a residential zone, maintenance of the residential appearance of the facility. It also could include limits on the number of staff personnel. *See* CONGREGATE HOUSING.

BOARDING HOUSE

A dwelling or part thereof, in which lodging is provided by the owner or operator to more than three boarders.

Comment: The necessary distinction is between a boarding home and a hotel or motel. The difference is that a boarding home is a dwelling while a motel or hotel is a commercial establishment licensed by the municipality and often by the state to accept transients. Some problems may arise, however, in terms of recent court decisions relating to what constitutes a family. The most recent case in New Jersey, the *State* v. *Baker* (158 N.J. Super 536 [App. Div. 1978]) blurs this distinction. Municipalities may establish whatever number of boarders constitutes a boarding house. Anything less would be permitted as a matter of right in any residence.

BOARDING STABLE

A structure designed for the feeding, housing and exercising of horses not owned by the owner of the premises.

BOARDWALK

An elevated public pedestrian walkway constructed over a public street or along an ocean front or beach.

BOATEL

A combination of a motel and marina which is accessible to boats as well as automobiles and includes boat sales and servicing facilities, overnight accommodation for transients and eating and drinking facilities.

BOG

Wet, spongy land, usually poorly drained, highly acid and rich in plant residue.

BONUS ZONING

See INCENTIVE ZONING.

BOROUGH

A designation for an incorporated, self-governing municipality.

Comment: In some states, this same definition applies to all incorporated municipalities.

BRACKISH WATER

A mixture of fresh and salt water.

BREEDING FARM

A farm where animals are impregnated either directly or by artifical insemination.

BRIDGE

A structure having a clear span of more than twenty feet designed to convey vehicles and/or pedestrians over a watercourse, railroad, public or private right-of-way, or any depression.

Comment: Structures having a clear span of less than 20 feet are usually designated as culverts.

39

BRITISH THERMAL UNIT (BTU)

A unit of heat equal to 252 calories which is the quantity of heat required to raise temperature of one pound of water one degree Fahrenheit.

BROADCAST APPLICATION

The application of a chemical over an entire field, lawn or other area.

BROOK

A small stream or creek.

BUFFER STRIP

Land area used to visibly separate one use from another or to shield or block noise, lights, or other nuisances. *See Figure 2.*

Comment: Buffer strips may be required to include fences or berms, as well as shrubs and trees.

BUFFER ZONE

See TRANSITION ZONE.

BUILDABLE AREA

The area of a lot remaining after the minimum yard and open space requirements of the zoning ordinance have been met. *See Figure 20.*

Comment: Ordinances also may exclude other areas from the buildable area such as easements, critical areas and flood plains.

BUILDING

Any structure having a roof supported by columns or walls and intended for the shelter, housing or enclosure of any individual, animal, process, equipment, goods or materials of any kind or nature.

BUILDING, ACCESSORY

A subordinate structure on the same lot as the principal or main building or use occupied or devoted to a use incidental to the principal use.

BUILDING COVERAGE

The horizontal area measured within the outside of the exterior walls of the ground floor of all principal and accessory buildings on a lot. *See Figure 20.*

Comment: In single-family residential structures, porches and decks usually are excluded. For multifamily and nonresidential structures, a more meaningful control over the intensity and environmental impact of development are limits on impervious surfaces and floor area ratio, coupled with open space requirements.

40

BUILDING HEIGHT

The vertical distance of a building measured from the average elevation of the finished grade within twenty feet of the structure to the highest point of the roof. *See Figure 3.*

Comment: Building heights usually exclude penthouses containing mechanical equipment such as air conditioning or elevator equipment and church spires, water towers, radio antennas, etc. The provision for measuring the finished lot grade within 20 feet of the structure is to prevent the deliberately building up of a portion of the site on which the building will sit in order to permit an additional story to be constructed. *See* HEIGHT.

 BUILDING INSPECTOR

That individual designated by the appointing authority to enforce the provisions of the building code.

 **BUILDING LINE**

A line parallel to the street line at a distance therefrom equal to the depth of the front yard required for the zoning district in which the lot is located. *See* SETBACK LINE. *See Figure 20.*

 BUILDING PERMIT

Written permission issued by the proper municipal authority for the construction, repair, alteration or addition to a structure.

 BUILDING, PRINCIPAL

A building in which is conducted the principal use of the lot on which it is located. *See Figure 22.*

 **BUILT-UP AREA**

An area where less than twenty-five percent of the land is vacant.

Comment: While the figure of 25% is somewhat arbitrary, it is at this figure (75% developed), that an area gives the observer the impression of being substantially developed.

 BULK ENVELOPE

See ZONING ENVELOPE.

 BULKHEAD

A retaining wall created along a body of water behind which fill is placed.

 BULK PLANE

See SKY EXPOSURE PLANE.

 BULK REGULATIONS

Standards that control the height, density, intensity and location of structures.

41

BULK STORAGE

The storage of chemicals, petroleum products and other materials in above-ground containers for subsequent resale to distributors or retail dealers or outlets.

Comment: Bulk storage is essentially a warehousing operation. The key portion of the definition is that the products are sold for eventual resale and not directly to the consuming public.

BULKHEAD LINE

A line along a navigable water offshore from which no fill or structure is permitted.

Comment: The bulkhead line defines the permanent shore line of navigable waterways or lakes. The top is usually stated in feet above sea level.

BULLETIN BOARD SIGN

See SIGN, BULLETIN BOARD.

BUMPERS

Permanent devices in each parking stall which block the front wheels of a vehicle. *See Figure 2.*

Comment: Bumpers can be a problem in that they crack frequently and make it difficult to clear parking areas of snow. They also trap debris and papers. A better arrangement is to install curbing around the peripheral parking spaces and permit the cars to overhang the curbing.

BUS SHELTER

A small, roofed structure, having from one to three walls, located near a street, and designed primarily for the protection and convenience of bus passengers. *See Figure 13.*

BUS TERMINAL or STATION

Any premises for the transient housing or parking of motor-driven buses and the loading and unloading of passengers.

BUS TURNOUT

A paved indentation at the side of a roadway designed to allow buses to pick up and discharge passengers. *See Figure 13.*

BUSINESS SERVICES

Establishments primarily engaged in rendering services to business establishments on a fee or contract basis, such as advertising and mailing; building maintenance; employment service; management and consulting services; protective services; equipment rental and leasing;

commercial research; development and testing; photo finishing; and personal supply services.

BUSINESS SIGN   *See* SIGN, BUSINESS.

BUSWAY   A vehicular right-of-way or portion thereof which is reserved exclusively for the use of buses.

Comment: The exclusive reservation may be limited to peak traffic hours.

C

 **CALIPER**   The diameter of a tree trunk.

Comment: The diameter should be specified and indicate where measured from ground level. The standard, which may be used to require certain mature trees to remain on a site or require planting of minimum age trees, will vary with the species. Certain trees are normally thinner, such as birches or dogwoods, and consequently the standard would be different than for other species.

 **CAMPER**   Any individual who occupies a campsite or otherwise assumes charge of, or is placed in charge of, a campsite.

CAMPGROUND   A plot of ground upon which two or more campsites are located, established or maintained for occupancy by camping units of the general public as temporary living quarters for recreation, education or vacation purposes.

Comment: Most states regulate campgrounds under a state campground code or sanitary code. Any state definitions should be used in the local ordinance. The state code also may prescribe minimum standards, including the amount of space required for each campsite, provision of sanitary facilities, etc. Local ordinance provisions usually are required to be as strict as the state's but in some states, they may be stricter. Many state or local ordinances also establish a minimum period of time, fifteen days or more in a calendar year, to qualify as a campground.

43

CAMPING UNIT — Any tent, trailer, cabin, lean-to or similar structure established or maintained and operated in a camp ground as temporary living quarters for recreation, education or vacation purposes.

Comment: Ordinances usually exclude the camping unit kept by the owner of land and occupied as a dwelling. It often excludes camping units which are not occupied and kept at the campground for storage purposes in areas reserved for such vehicles or units.

CAMPING VEHICLE — *See* RECREATIONAL VEHICLE.

CAMPSITE — Any plot of ground within a campground intended for the exclusive occupancy by a camping unit or units under the control of a camper.

CAMPUS — The grounds and building of a public or private college, university, school or institution.

CANAL — An artificial waterway for transportation or irrigation.

CANDLEPOWER — Luminous intensity expressed in candelas.

Comment: Candlepower is a measure of illuminating power which has generally been replaced by the foot-candle. For those technically inclined, the luminous intensity is the luminous flux per unit solid angle in a given direction. *See* FOOTCANDLE.

CANOPY — *See* AWNING.

CAPITAL IMPROVEMENT — A government acquisition of real property, major construction project, or acquisition of long lasting, expensive equipment.

Comment: Capital improvements are usually large, non-recurring items. Many ordinances place a minimum expenditure of $2,500 to qualify as a capital improvement.

CAPITAL IMPROVE-MENTS PROGRAM — A proposed timetable or schedule of all future capital improvements to be carried out during a specific period and listed in order of priority, together with cost estimates and the anticipated means of financing each project.

44

Comment: The capital improvements program is usually a six-year program with the first year being the capital improvements budget.

CAR WASH

See AUTOMATIC CAR WASH and AUTOMOBILE WASH.

CARBON DIOXIDE (CO2)

A colorless, odorless, nonpoisonous gas that is a normal part of the ambient air and which is a product of fossil fuel combustion.

CARBON MONOXIDE (CO)

A colorless, odorless, highly toxic gas that is a normal byproduct of incomplete fossil fuel combustion.

CARPOOL, CARPOOLING

A single vehicle, share-the-expense method of transportation for two or more individuals who regularly travel together to a common destination.

Comment: Carpooling resembles vanpooling but differs in one major respect; under carpooling the driver is usually the car owner. In vanpooling, the vehicle is usually owned by the employer and the driver rides free in return for maintaining the van and serving as driver. In addition, companies who operate vans under a formal vanpooling program are eligible for certain federal grants and tax benefits.

CARPORT

A roofed structure providing space for the parking or storage of motor vehicles and enclosed on not more than three sides.

CARRY-OUT RESTAURANT

An establishment which by design of physical facilities or by service or packaging procedures permits or encourages the purchase of prepared ready-to-eat foods intended primarily to be consumed off the premises, and where the consumption of food in motor vehicles on the premises is not permitted or not encouraged.

CARTWAY

That area of a street within which vehicles are permitted, including travel lanes and parking areas but not including shoulders, curbs, sidewalks or swales.

CASINO

A room or rooms in which legal gaming is conducted.

CATALYTIC CONVERTER

An air pollution abatement device that removes organic contaminants by oxidizing them into carbon dioxide and water through chemical reaction and is used to reduce nitrogen oxide emissions from motor vehicles.

 **CATCH BASIN**

An inlet designed to intercept and redirect surface waters.

CELLAR

A space with less than one-half of its floor-to-ceiling height above the average finished grade of the adjoining ground or with a floor-to-ceiling height of less than 6½ feet. *See Figure 3.*

Comment: Cellars should be used only for mechanical equipment accessory to the principal structure or for nonhabitable space such as a recreation or storage area. As such they are not counted as a story or in the computation of the intensity of land use development.

CELLS

With respect to solid waste disposal, earthen compartments in which solid wastes are dumped, compacted and covered over daily with layers of earth.

CEMETERY

Property used for the interring of the dead.

Comment: Most development ordinances do not include provisions for cemeteries. They are so unique a use that they are generally handled by variance. In communities where there are cemeteries which are regulated in the development ordinance, there should be some consideration as to whether or not to allow for mausoleums where the bodies are interred above ground in stacked vaults. In areas with high water tables this is a fairly common type of burial. Some of the newer mausoleums may be up to ten stories high and some care should be used in locating these away from the periphery of the cemeteries.

CENSUS

An official periodic enumeration of a designated geographic area's population and its characteristics.

CENSUS TRACT

Small areas into which large cities and adjacent areas have been divided for statistical purposes.

CENTRAL BUSINESS DISTRICT (CBD)

The major shopping area within a city usually containing, in addition to retail uses, governmental offices, service uses, professional, cultural, recreational and entertainment establishments and uses, residences, hotels and motels, appropriate industrial activities, and transportation facilities.

Comment: There is no hard and fast rule as to what the central business district may include. In fact, all uses are appropriate providing they do not adversely infringe on other uses or diminish the traditional retail, office, cultural and entertainment functions. Controls on industry in the CBD, for example, might restrict them from prime, first-floor locations which normally would be used for retail activities. Even open space and passive and active recreational facilities have a place in the CBD.

CERTIFICATE OF COMPLIANCE

A document issued by the proper authority that the plans for a proposed use meets all applicable codes and regulations.

CERTIFICATE OF NEED

A required document which must be obtained before certain facilities can be constructed or expanded.

Comment: Certificates of need usually are associated with health facilities where the regional health facilities planning council is required to establish the need before a new or expanded facility can be constructed. However, certificates of need also are required for subsidized housing facilities and may be a condition for certain other public uses.

CERTIFICATE OF OCCUPANCY (CO)

A document issued by the proper authority allowing the occupancy or use of a building and certifying that the structure or use has been constructed or will be used in compliance with all the applicable municipal codes and ordinances.

CERTIFICATION

A written statement by the appropriate officer that required constructions, inspections, tests or notices have been performed and comply with applicable requirements.

CESSION DEED

The conveyance to a local governmental body of private property street rights.

CESSPOOL

A covered pit with open jointed lining where untreated sewage is discharged, the liquid portion of which is disposed of by seepage or leeching into the surrounding porous soil, the solids or sludge being retained in the pit.

CFS

Cubic feet per second.

Comment: The measure of the amount of liquid or gas passing a given point.

47

 CHAIN

A lineal measure equal to 66 feet.

Comment: This surveyor's measure is no longer in use. Many street right-of-way widths were laid out as 33 feet, or ½ chain.

CHAIN STORE

Retail outlets with the same name, selling similar types of merchandise, operating under a common merchandising policy and usually owned or franchised by a single corporate entity.

CHANGE OF USE

Any use which substantially differs from the previous use of a building or land.

Comment: Change of use is important in that any such change usually requires site plan approval. New Jersey courts have indicated that change of occupancy or change of ownership shall not be construed as change of use. The change of use has to be substantially different from the previous use. Thus, a retail clothing store selling men's clothes would not be substantially different from a retail clothing store selling women's clothes. Whether a retail clothing store would be substantially different from a drug store is debatable. One possibility which has not, to the best of our knowledge, yet been tried, is to define "substantially different" as "a use which is outside the group number classification of the previous use as set forth in the Standard Industrial Classification Manual." For example, under major group #59, Miscellaneous Retail, group #594 includes miscellaneous shopping goods stores. This three-number group includes sporting goods establishments, bookstores, stationery stores, jewelry stores, hobby, toy and games, camera and photography supplies, gift novelty, and souvenir shops. Any use within group #594 would be considered substantially the same as any other within that group. Any use in another three-numbered group would be considered substantially different.

CHANNEL

A watercourse with a definite bed and banks which confine and conduct the normal continuous or intermittent flow of water.

CHANNELIZATION

(1) The straightening and deepening of channels and/or the surfacing thereof to permit water to move rapidly and/or directly; (2) A traffic control device which forces vehicles into certain traffic flows or turning movements.

48

CHARITABLE USE

Property used by a nonprofit or eleemosynary organization that provides a service beneficial to the general public or to a significant portion of the public for no fee or at a fee recognized as being less than that charged by profit-making organizations.

CHATTEL

Personal property as contrasted with real estate.

 CHEMICAL OXYGEN DEMAND (COD)

A measure of the amount of oxygen required to oxidize organic and oxidizable inorganic compounds in water.

Comment: The COD test, like the BOD test, is used to determine the degree of pollution in an effluent.

CHILD CARE CENTER

A private establishment enrolling four or more children between 2 and 5 years of age and where tuition, fees, or other forms of compensation for the care of the children is charged, and which is licensed or approved to operate as a child care center.

Comment: Child care centers usually are licensed by state agencies and must meet certain criteria. As women have become an increasing part of the work force, conveniently located child care centers generally are considered permitted uses in residential zones.

CHIMNEY

A structure containing one or more flues for drawing off emissions from stationary sources of combustion.

CHLORINATED HYDROCARBONS

A class of generally long-lasting, broad-spectrum insecticides.

Comment: The best known of the chlorinated hydrocarbons is DDT, first used for insect control during World War II. The qualities of persistence and effectiveness against a wide variety of insect pests were long regarded as highly desirable in agriculture, public health and home uses. But later research has revealed that these same qualities may represent a potential hazard through accumulation in the food chain and persistence in the environment.

CHLORINATION

The application of chlorine to drinking water, sewage or industrial waste for disinfection or oxidation of undesirable compounds.

CHLORINATOR A device for adding a chlorine-containing gas or liquid to drinking or waste water.

CHLOROSIS Yellowing or whitening of normally green plant parts caused by disease organisms, lack of oxygen or nutrients in the soil or by various air pollutants.

CHRISTMAS TREE FARM A land area cultivated for the growing of trees harvested and marketed for Christmas trees.

CHURCH A building or structure, or groups of buildings or structures, which by design and construction are primarily intended for the conducting of organized religious services and accessory uses associated therewith.

Comment: The major problem associated with churches and other places of worship is that very often the accessory uses may create greater impact than the primary use. Places of worship, for example, may have attendant schools, meeting halls, and kitchens capable of feeding many hundreds of persons. They often are rented out for weddings and other social events. In previous years, churches drew primarily from the neighborhood in which they were located. Today, the area of service may be considerably larger. Care should be given in drafting any ordinance regulating places of worship to insure that the accessory uses do not become nuisances. Adequate setbacks are required and parking should be provided for all the uses contemplated.

Some places of worship do enjoy greater popularity during certain holidays. While it is not necessary to plan for peak use, there should be some consideration given to the several holidays or holy days within the year when occupancy will be two-to-three times that of normal worship services.

CIRCULATION Systems, structures and physical improvements for the movement of people, goods, water, air, sewage, or power by such means as streets, highways, railways, waterways, towers, airways, pipes and conduits, and the handling of people and goods by such means as terminals, stations, warehouses, and other storage buildings or transshipment points.

CISTERN A tank or reservoir used for storing rain water.

50

 **CITIZEN PARTICIPATION**

Public involvement in governmental policy formation and implementation.

 **CITY PLANNING**

The decisionmaking process in which goals and objectives are established, existing resources and conditions analyzed, strategies developed, and controls enacted to achieve the goals and objectives as they relate to cities and communities.

CIVIC CENTER

A building or complex of buildings that house municipal offices and services, and which may include cultural, recreational, athletic, convention and entertainment facilities owned and/or operated by a governmental agency.

CLARIFICATION

In waste water treatment, the removal of turbidity and suspended solids by settling, often aided by centrifugal action and chemically induced coagulation.

CLARIFIER

In waste water treatment, a settling tank which mechanically removes solids that settle from water.

CLEAN AIR ACT

A federal act establishing national air quality standards.

CLINIC

An establishment where patients are admitted for examination and treatment by one or more physicians, dentists, psychologists or social workers and where patients are not usually lodged overnight.

CLOVERLEAF

A multiple highway intersection usually in the form of a four leaf clover, which, by means of curving ramps from one level to another, permits traffic to move or turn in any of four directions without interference. *See Figure 32.*

CLUB

A group of people organized for a common purpose to pursue common goals, interests or activities and usually characterized by certain membership qualifications, payment of fees and dues, regular meetings, and a constitution and by-laws.

Comment: Typically, clubs were usually permitted in residential neighborhoods under the phrase, "clubs, lodges and social buildings." These clubs were related to the neighborhood in terms of the ethnic, religious or cultural characteristics of the residents. Today, clubs have become much more regionally oriented and consequently, there's probably little reason to locate them in residential areas. A distinction also should be made between bona fide clubs and those which usually are commercial in nature, such as tennis and racquetball clubs which are owned by individuals and operated for a profit. *See* FRATERNAL ORGANIZATION.

 **CLUBHOUSE**

A building, or portion thereof, used by a club.

CLUSTER

A development design technique that concentrates buildings in specific areas on the site to allow the remaining land to be used for recreation, common open space, and preservation of environmentally sensitive features.

CLUSTER SUBDIVISION

A form of development for single-family residential subdivisions that permits a reduction in lot area and bulk requirements, provided there is no increase in the number of lots permitted under a conventional subdivision and the resultant land area is devoted to open space. *See Figure 36.*

Comment: The cluster subdivision is an excellent planning concept that has been used successfully in many communities. Using this concept the number of lots (density) remains the same as in a conventional development but the community gains in the retention of open space and reduced maintenance costs by having shorter streets and utility lines. The developer also gains in reduced development costs, which may result in less costly housing. Many communities require the developer to submit two sketch plans before approving a cluster subdivision; a conventional subdivision plat to establish the number of *developable* lots possible and a cluster subdivision plat to determine the appropriateness of cluster design for the site.

COHABITATION

Households which contain two unrelated adults of the opposite sex.

COLIFORM INDEX

An index of the purity of water based on a count of its coliform bacteria.

COLIFORM ORGANISM

Any of a number of organisms common to the intestinal tract of humans and animals whose presence in waste water is an indication of pollution and of potentially dangerous bacterial contamination.

COLLEGE	An educational institution authorized by the state to award baccalaureate or higher degrees.
COLLIERY	A coal mine, its buildings and equipment.
COLOSSEUM	A large enclosed and roofed structure used for spectator sports and exhibitions.
COMBINED SEWERS	A sewerage system that carries both sanitary sewage and stormwater runoff.
COMBUSTION	Burning.

Comment: Technically, combustion is a rapid oxidation accompanied by the release of energy in the form of heat and light. To reduce air pollution, many states or communities now prohibit outdoor burning.

COMMERCIAL CONDOMINIUM	*See* CONDOMINIUM.
COMMERCIAL GARAGE	*See* GARAGE, PUBLIC.
COMMERCIAL GREENHOUSE	A structure in which plants, vegetables, flowers and similar materials are grown for sale.
COMMERCIAL USE	Activity carried out for pecuniary gain.
COMMERCIAL VEHICLE	Any motor vehicle licensed by the state as a commercial vehicle.

Comment: The parking or storage of commercial vehicles is usually restricted in residential zones. Current practice is to permit exceptions to certain kinds of commercial vehicles in these zones. For example, a passenger vehicle licensed as a commercial vehicle could be permitted as could a van of up to a certain carrying capacity.

COMMINUTION   Mechanical shredding or pulverizing of waste, converting it into a homogenous and more manageable material.

Comment: Used in solid waste management and in the primary stage of waste water treatment.

COMMINUTOR   A device that grinds solids to make them easier to treat.

53

 COMMON
ELEMENTS

Land amenities, parts of buildings, central services and utilities, and any other elements and facilities owned and used by all condominium unit owners and designated in the master deed as common elements.

 COMMON
OPEN SPACE

See OPEN SPACE, COMMON.

 COMMON
OWNERSHIP

Ownership by one or more individuals in any form of ownership, of two or more contiguous lots.

 COMMON
PASSAGEWAY

A commonly shared or used pedestrian or vehicular way that connects or serves two or more properties. *See* PARTY DRIVEWAY.

 COMMUNICATION
USE

Establishments furnishing point-to-point communication services whether by wire or radio, either aurally or visually, including radio and television broadcasting and the exchange or recording of messages.

 COMMUNITY
ASSOCIATION

A homeowners association organized to own, maintain, and operate common facilities and to enhance and protect their common interests.

 COMMUNITY
CENTER

A building used for recreational, social, educational and cultural activities, usually owned and operated by a public or nonprofit group or agency.

 COMMUNITY
FACILITY

A building or structure owned and operated by a governmental agency to provide a governmental service to the public.

 COMMUNITY
IMPACT STUDY

See IMPACT ANALYSIS.

 COMPACTION

Reducing the bulk of solid waste by rolling, tamping and compression.

 COMPLETE
APPLICATION

An application form completed as specified by ordinance and the rules and regulations of the municipal agency and all accompanying documents required by ordinance for approval of the application.

Comment: An application should be certified as complete immediately upon the meeting of all requirements specified in the ordinance and in the rules and regulations of the municipal agency. On the day it is so certified by the administrative officer, the time period for action by the municipal agency begins. Problems occasionally occur when a required document upon initial review does not appear to substantially meet the ordinance requirements. For example, a landscaping plan showing only foundation plants surrounding a building on a ten-acre site may be rejected outright as incomplete. However, a better way to handle questionable submissions is to accept them in terms of a complete application but, after detailed review, to reject the questionable or unacceptable element as not in conformance with the technical or design standards set forth in the ordinance.

COMPOST

Relatively stable decomposed organic material.

COMPOSTING

A controlled process of degrading organic matter by microorganisms.

Comment: Composting may be achieved by several methods: (1) Mechanical—a method in which the compost is continuously and mechanically mixed and aerated; (2) Ventilated cell—compost is mixed and aerated by being dropped through a vertical series of ventilated cells; (3) Windrow—an open-air method in which compostable material is placed in windrows, piles or ventilated bins or pits and occasionally turned or mixed. The process may be anerobic or aerobic.

COMPREHENSIVE PLAN

See MASTER PLAN.

CONCEPT PLAN

See PLAT, SKETCH.

CONDEMNATION

The exercise by a governmental agency of the right of eminent domain. *See* EMINENT DOMAIN.

CONDITIONAL USE

A use permitted in a particular zoning district only upon showing that such use in a specified location will comply with all the conditions and standards for the location or operation of such use as specified in a zoning ordinance and authorized by the planning board.

Comment: Conditional uses are often referred to as special permit uses. In some states, the board of adjustment is the agency which grants the conditional use, while in others it is the planning board.

 **CONDITIONAL USE PERMIT**

A permit issued by the authorized board stating that the conditional use meets all conditions set forth in local ordinances.

 **CONDOMINIUM**

A building, or group of buildings, in which units are owned individually, and the structure, common areas and facilities are owned by all the owners on a proportional, undivided basis.

Comment: By definition, a condominium has common areas and facilities and there is an association of owners organized for the purpose of maintaining, administering and operating the common areas and facilities. It is a legal form of ownership of real estate and not a specific building style. The purchaser has title to his or her interior space in the building and an undivided interest in parts of the interior, the exterior, and other common elements. The property is identified in a master deed and recorded on a plat with the local jurisdiction. The common elements usually include the land underneath and surrounding the building, certain improvements on the land, and such items as plumbing, wiring, and major utility systems, the interior areas between walls, the public interior spaces, exterior walls, streets and recreational facilities.

 **CONDOMINIUM ASSOCIATION**

The community association which administers and maintains the common property and common elements of a condominium.

Comment: Condominium associations differ from other forms of community associations in that the condominium association does not have title to the common property and facilities. These are owned by the condominium owner on a proportional, undivided basis.

CONDOMINIUM, COMMERCIAL

A building (or group of buildings) used for office, businesses, professional services and other commercial enterprise organized, owned and maintained as a condominium.

CONDOMINIUM HOTEL

A condominium set up like a hotel in which each room is individually owned and in which some or all rooms are available to transients for rent.

CONDOMINIUM, INDUSTRIAL

An industrial building (or group of buildings) organized, owned and maintained as a condominium.

CONDOMINIUM, OFFICE

An office building (or group of buildings) organized, owned and maintained as a condominium.

CONFERENCE CENTER

A facility used for business or professional conferences and seminars, often with accommodations for sleeping, eating and recreation.

Comment: Communities face the decision whether or not to allow conference centers to rent rooms and facilities to transients. Very often a specific percentage of rooms must be devoted to conference use and only a small percentage of rooms must be devoted to conference use and only a small percentage can be made available for transient trade.

CONGREGATE HOUSING

A dwelling providing shelter and services for the elderly which may include meals, housekeeping, and personal care assistance.

Comment: Congregate housing provides a residential environment for the elderly who may be functionally impaired or socially isolated, but otherwise in good health. The residents can maintain a semi-independent lifestyle and do not require more intensive care as provided in an intensive care facility such as a nursing home. *See* BOARDING HOME FOR SHELTERED CARE.

CONSERVATION DISTRICT

See SOIL CONSERVATION DISTRICT.

CONSERVATION EASEMENT

See EASEMENT, CONSERVATION.

CONSIDERATION

An inducement to a contract.

CONSOLIDATION

The removal of lot lines between contiguous parcels.

Comment: Consolidation of several lots into a single lot or tract usually is considered an exempt subdivision. *See* ASSEMBLAGE and SUBDIVISION.

CONSTRUCTION OFFICIAL

See BUILDING INSPECTOR.

CONSTRUCTION PERMIT

A permit required for the erection, alteration, or extension of a structure.

57

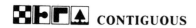 **CONTIGUOUS**

Next to, abutting, or touching and having a boundary, or portion thereof, which is coterminous. *See* ABUT and ADJOINING LOT OR LAND.

 **CONTINUING EASEMENT**

See EASEMENT, CONTINUING.

CONVENTION FACILITY

A building or portion thereof designed to accommodate three hundred or more people in assembly.

Comment: The definition is admittedly broad, and the figure 300 is somewhat arbitrary. It is designed to give the municipality as much control over these very intensive uses as possible. In the zones where they are permitted, standards will then have to be established relating to parking, setbacks, signs, etc.

CONVENTIONAL ENERGY SYSTEM

Any energy system, including supply elements, furnaces, burners, tanks, boilers, related controls, and energy-distribution components, which uses any source(s) of energy other than solar energy.

Comment: The sources of conventional energy systems include the usual fossil fuels such as gas, oil, coal, as well as nuclear fuels. They do not include windmills.

CONVERSION

A change in the use of land or a structure.

COOLING TOWER

A device to remove excess heat from water used in industrial operations, notably in electric power generation.

CORNER LOT

See LOT, CORNER.

COST-BENEFIT ANALYSIS

An analytic method whereby the actual and hidden costs of a proposed project are measured against the benefits to be received from the project.

Comment: The field of cost-benefit analysis is complex and ill defined. For example, some cost-benefit analyses talk only in terms of primary costs. Others may include secondary and tertiary costs as well as benefits. For additional information, the reader is referred to Robert W. Burchell and David Listokin, *Fiscal Impact Handbook* (New Brunswick, N.J.: Center for Urban Policy Research, 1978).

COTTAGE

A small, detached dwelling unit.

Comment: A cottage is usually an outbuilding on a larger tract of land. Often it is seasonal and lacks heat, but for various reasons, may have been converted to an all-year-round dwelling. Local ordinances should specify minimum standards for space, heating and sanitary facilities as a condition of conversion.

COTTAGE INDUSTRY

A home occupation carried out in a structure separate from the principal building.

Comment: Cottage industry is a term previously used to describe manufacturing and assembly carried out in the home, often on a contract basis with the entire family working. In later years, cottage industry was accessory to the principal residential use and usually carried out in an outbuilding or accessory structure. It is now occasionally used to describe home occupations.

COUNCIL OF GOVERNMENTS

A regional planning and review authority whose membership includes representation from all communities in the designated region.

COUNTRY CLUB

A land area and buildings containing recreational facilities, clubhouse and usual accessory uses, open only to members and their guests for a membership fee.

Comment: The question faced by communities is whether or not to allow country clubs to lease out their facilities to outsiders for banquets, weddings, etc. These outside activities, while similar in nature to what would normally be permitted to club members, do intensify the use. On the other hand, they allow the clubs to make money and very often are the difference between continuing the primary country club use or being forced to sell for development.

COUNTY MASTER PLAN

The official master plan for the physical development of a county.

COURT

Any open space, unobstructed from ground to sky, other than a yard, that is on the same lot with and bounded on two or more sides by the walls of a building. *See* PLAZA and SQUARE. *See Figure 13.*

COURT, INNER

An open area, unobstructed from the ground to the sky which is bounded on more than three sides by the exterior walls of one or more buildings. *See Figure 4.*

COURT, OUTER

An open area, unobstructed from the ground to the sky, which is bounded on not more than three sides by the exterior walls of one or more buildings. *See Figure 4.*

COVE

A small bay or inlet or a sheltered recess in a cliff face.

COVENANT

See RESTRICTIVE COVENANT.

COVER MATERIAL

Soil that is used to cover compacted solid waste in a sanitary landfill.

COVERAGE

See LOT COVERAGE.

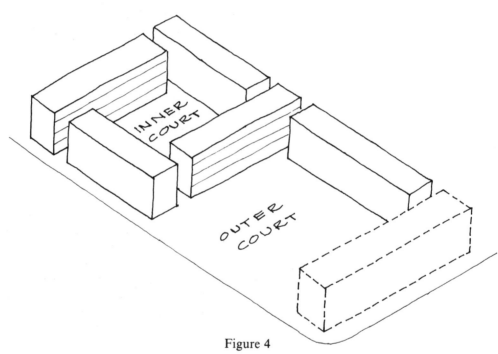

Figure 4

CRAWL SPACE

A space between the ceiling of one story and floor of the next story, which usually contains pipes, ducts, wiring and lighting fixtures and permits access but is too low for an individual to stand. *See Figure 3.*

Comment: The crawl space may be a cellar area no more than 4½ feet high, or, if between a ceiling and a flat or shed roof, a cockloft.

60

 **CREEK**

A small stream somewhat larger than a brook.

CRITICAL AREA

An area with one or more of the following characteristics: (1) slopes in excess of twenty percent; (2) floodplain; (3) soils classified as having a high water table; (4) soils classified as highly erodible, subject to erosion or highly acidic; (5) land incapable of meeting percolation requirements; (6) land formerly used for landfill operations or hazardous industrial use; (7) fault areas; (8) stream corridors; (9) estuaries; (10) mature stands of native vegetation; (11) aquifer recharge and discharge areas.

Comment: The purpose of classifying certain lands as critical areas is to focus attention on these lands and to establish additional requirements before development can take place. The additional requirements may include the preparation and submission of an environmental impact statement or requiring the applicant to specifically address what measures will be taken with respect to the critical elements.

CROP

A harvestable product, planted, grown and cultivated in the soil.

CUBIC CONTENT

The area of space contained within the walls of a room or building found by multiplying the height, width and length.

CUL-DE-SAC

The turnaround at the end of a dead-end street.

Comment: The term cul-de-sac is often used to describe the street itself which is further defined as a street with only a single means of ingress and egress and having a turnaround. *See* STREET, CUL-DE-SAC and STREET, DEAD-END.

CULTURAL EUTROPHICATION

Acceleration by humans of the natural aging process of bodies of water.

Comment: Eutrophication often takes place because of runoff from cultivated lawns or the use of septic systems that introduce nutrients into the water, thus hastening the growth of algae and underwater plants.

61

◨ CULTURAL FACILITIES — Establishments such as museums, art galleries, botanical and zoological gardens of an historic, educational or cultural interest which are not operated commercially.

Comment: While these activities may charge admission fees, the bulk of their expenses are borne by public agencies, foundations, or donations.

▶▛▲ CULVERT — A drain, ditch or conduit not incorporated in a closed system, that carries drainage water under a driveway, roadway, railroad, pedestrian walk or publicway.

▶▛ CURB — A stone or concrete boundary usually marking the edge of the roadway or paved area.

▶▛ CURB CUT — The opening along the curb line at which point vehicles may enter or leave the roadway. *See Figure 2.*

▶▛ CURB LEVEL — The permanently established grade of the curb top in front of a lot.

▶▛ CURB RETURN — The connecting link between the street curb and the ramp curb.

▲ CURRENT — The part of any body of water that has more or less steady flow in a definite direction for certain periods during the day.

◨▶▛▲ CURRENT PLANNING CAPACITY — A measure of the ability of a region to accommodate the growth and development within the limits defined by existing infrastructure and natural resource capabilities.

Comment: Current planning capacity (CPC) is currently finding vogue in a number of zoning ordinances. The Ramapo, N.Y., Zoning Ordinance awards points for various infrastructure improvements and subtracts them when certain environmental constraints are noted. The higher the number of points, the higher the permitted development density. Generally, CPC is defined by water supply, water and air quality, sewage capability, highway capacity and community facilities.

▶▛ CURVILINEAR STREET SYSTEM — A pattern of streets which is curved. *See Figure 34.*

▶▛▲ CUT — A portion of land surface or area from which earth has been removed or will be removed by excavation; the depth below the original ground surface or excavated surface. *See Figure 21.*

D

DATUM

A reference point, line or plane used as a basis for measurements.

DATUM PLANE

A surface used for reference from which heights or depths are calculated.

DAY CARE CENTER/ DAY NURSERY

See CHILD CARE CENTER.

DDT

The first of the modern chlorinated hydrocarbon insecticides. Its chemical name is 1,1,1-tricholoro-2,2-bis (p-chloriphenyl)-ethane.

Comment: See comment under CHLORINATED HYDRO-CARBONS.

DEAD END STREET

See STREET, DEAD END.

DECELERATION LANE

An added roadway lane that permits cars to slow down and leave the main vehicle stream. *See Figure 1.*

DECIBEL

A unit of sound pressure level.

Comment: The decibel (abbreviated dB) is used to express noise level and a reference quantity is implied. The reference level is a sound pressure of 20 micronewtons per square meter. Zero decibels, the starting point of the scale of noise level, is about the level of the weakest sound that can be heard by someone with very good hearing in an extremely quiet location. The noise level in an average residence is about 50 decibels; 20 feet from a subway train the noise level is about 90 decibels; and 200 feet from a jet, about 120 decibels.

DECIDUOUS

Plants that drop their leaves before becoming dormant in winter.

Comment: In specifying any buffer areas, there should be a mix of deciduous and evergreen trees with the predominant emphasis on evergreens, which of course provide an all-year-round buffer.

63

 **DECK LINE**

The intersection of two roof surfaces of a mansard roof forming the highest horizontal line of the steeper roof slope. *See Figure 28.*

 **DECOMPOSITION**

Reduction of the net energy level and change in chemical composition of organic matter because of the actions of aerobic or anaerobic microorganisms.

 **DEDICATION**

Gift or donation of property by the owner to another party.

Comment: Such transfer is conveyed by written instrument and is completed with an acceptance. The dedication is often for a specific use.

 **DEED**

A legal document conveying ownership of real property.

DEED RESTRICTION

See RESTRICTIVE COVENANT.

DEMOGRAPHY

The study of population and its characteristics.

DEMOLITION (PERMIT)

A permit issued by a municipality before a building or structure or major part thereof is razed.

 **DENSITY**

The number of families, individuals, dwelling units, or housing structures per unit of land.

Comment: Ordinances regulating density must make it clear as to whether the standard is stated in net or gross density. Gross density includes all the land within the boundaries of the particular area excluding nothing. Net density excludes certain areas such as streets, easements, water areas, lands with environmental constraints, etc. (*See* NET AREA OF LOT). The exclusions have to be spelled out carefully. Some typical optimum densities for various types of housing are:

Type of Unit	Optimum Density Range (per gross acre)
Single-family detached	1-5 units
Two-family	6-10 units
Townhouse	6-8 units
Garden apartments	10-18 units
Mid-rise	25-30 units
High-rise	40-70 units

While units/acre is the most popular measurement of residential development because it is easy to use, a more accurate method in terms of community impact would be persons/acre or floor area ratio.

64

DENSITY MODIFICATION SUBDIVISION

See CLUSTER SUBDIVISION.

DESALINIZATION

Salt removed from sea or brackish water.

DESICCANT

A chemical agent that may be used to remove moisture from plants or insects causing them to wither and die.

DETENTION BASIN (POND)

A storage facility for the temporary storage of storm-water runoff.

Comment: Detention basins or ponds differ from retention basins in that the water storage is only temporary, often released by mechanical means at such time as downstream facilities can handle the flow. Usually, the basins are planted with grass and used for open space or recreation in periods of dry weather.

DETERGENT

A synthetic washing agent that, like soap, lowers the surface tension of water, emulsifies oils and holds dirt in suspension.

Comment: Environmentalists have criticized detergents containing large amounts of phosphorus-containing compounds that contribute to the eutrophication of waterways.

DETERIORATION

The marked diminishing of the physical condition of structures or buildings.

DEVELOPER

The legal or beneficial owner or owners of a lot or of any land included in a proposed development including the holder of an option or contract to purchase, or other persons having enforceable proprietary interests in such land.

DEVELOPMENT

The division of a parcel of land into two or more parcels; the construction, reconstruction, conversion, structural alteration, relocation or enlargement of any structure; any mining, excavation, landfill or land disturbance, and any use or extension of the use of land.

DEVELOPMENT ANALYSIS STUDY

An analysis of the alternative uses and potential alternative markets for a parcel of real estate.

65

 **DEVELOPMENT, CONVENTIONAL**

Development other than planned development or cluster development.

 **DEVELOPMENT, MAJOR**

Any development not a minor development.

 **DEVELOPMENT, MINOR**

Any development involving three or fewer lots and involving a land area of less than five acres and not requiring the extension of any new streets or other municipal or governmental facilities.

Comment: The definition of development as indicated previously is sufficiently broad to cover all types of activity relating to land and building. The designation of a minor development relieves the applicant of the need to meet the more stringent requirements of a major application including advertising, notification of neighbors, etc. The designation of three lots or less is strictly a local determination. In many built-up communities, where the streets and major infrastructure are already installed, five lots or less may be considered a minor subdivision. In urban areas, the five-acre standard for site plans may be too large and a smaller minimum may be desirable.

 **DEVELOPMENT, PLANNED**

See PLANNED DEVELOPMENT.

 **DEVELOPMENT REGULATION**

Zoning, subdivision, site plan, official map, flood plain regulation or other governmental regulation of the use and development of land.

 **DEVELOPMENT TIMING**

Regulating the rate and geographic sequence of development.

DIATOMACEOUS EARTH (DIATOMITE)

A fine siliceous material resembling chalk used in waste water treatment plants to filter sewage effluent to remove solids.

DIFFUSED AIR

A type of sewage aeration where air is pumped into the sewage through a perforated pipe.

DIGESTER

In a waste water treatment plant, a closed tank that decreases the volume of solids and stabilizes raw sludge by bacterial action.

▲ DIGESTION The biochemical decomposition of organic matter.

Comment: Digestion of sewage sludge takes place in tanks where the sludge decomposes, resulting in partial gasification, liquefaction and mineralization of pollutants.

▦▶▌▲ DILAPIDATION A deterioration of structures or buildings to the point of being unsafe or unfit for human habitation or use.

▲ DILUTION RATIO The ratio of the volume of water of a stream to the volume of incoming waste.

Comment: The capacity of a stream to accept waste water is partially dependent upon the dilution ratio.

▦ DISCOUNT CENTER A single store, or group of stores advertising a wide variety of merchandise for sale at less-than-retail cost.

▶▌▲ DISPOSAL AREA The entire area used for underground dispersion of the liquid portion of sewage.

Comment: Disposal area usually consists of the seepage pit or a disposal field or a combination of both.

▶▌▲ DISPOSAL BED That part of a disposal field for sanitary sewage.

Comment: A shallow area from which the entire earth contents have been removed and the excavation partially filled with satisfactory filtering material in which distribution lines have been laid and the entire area covered with topsoil and suitable vegetation cover.

▶▌▲ DISPOSAL FIELD An area consisting of a combination of disposal trenches and a disposal bed. *See Figure 30.*

Comment: The disposal field is used for dispersion of the liquid portion of sanitary sewage into the ground as close to the surface as possible.

▶▌▲ DISPOSAL TRENCH A shallow ditch with vertical sides and flat bottom partially filled with a satisfactory filtering material in which a single distribution line has been laid covered with topsoil and a suitable vegetative cover.

67

▲ DISSOLVED OXYGEN (DO)

The oxygen dissolved in water or sewage.

Comment: Adequate dissolved oxygen is necessary for the life of fish and other aquatic organisms. Low dissolved oxygen concentrations generally are due to discharge of excessive organic solids, the result of inadequate waste treatment.

▲ DISSOLVED SOLIDS

The total amount of dissolved material, organic and inorganic, contained in water or wastes.

Comment: Excessive dissolved solids make water unpalatable for drinking and unsuitable for industrial uses.

DISTANCE OF SIGN PROJECTION

The distance from the exterior wall surface of a building to the sign element farthest distance from such surface. *See Figure 29.*

DISTRIBUTION BOX

A water-tight structure that receives sanitary sewage effluent from a septic tank and distributes such sewage effluent in equal portions to two or more pipelines leading to the disposal field. *See Figure 30.*

DISTRIBUTION LINES

A series of open, jointed or perforated pipes used for the dispersion of sewage into disposal trenches or disposal beds. *See Figure 30.*

DISTRICT

A part, zone or geographic area within the municipality within which certain zoning or development regulations apply.

DIVERSION CHANNEL

A channel constructed across or at the bottom of a slope.

DOMICILE

A residence that is a permanent home to an individual.

DONATION

A voluntary gift for which no valuable consideration is given in exchange.

DORMER

A projection from a sloping roof which contains a window. *See Figure 26.*

DORMITORY

A building used as group living quarters for a student body or religious order as an accessory use for a college, university, boarding school, orphanage, convent, monastery or other similar institutional use.

Comment: Recent court cases on the definition of family (i.e., *State of N.J.* v. *Dennis Baker,* A-59, Supreme

68

Court of N.J.) makes the distinction between dormitories and households of unrelated individuals less precise. Regulations based on living space or other performance standard may offer the most positive method of control. *See* GROUP QUARTERS.

DOSE

In radiology, the quantity of absorbed energy or radiation.

DOSIMETER (DOSEMETER)

An instrument used to measure the amount of radiation an individual has received.

DOSING TANKS

A water-tight receptacle located between a septic tank and disposal area equipped with an automatic siphon device designed to discharge sewage intermittently into distribution lines in amounts proportional to the capacity of such line and to provide adequate rest periods between such discharges.

DOUBLE WIDE UNIT

Two mobile home units, attached side by side, which constitute the complete mobile home.

DOWN ZONE

To increase the intensity of use by increasing density or floor area ratio or otherwise decreasing bulk requirements.

DRAINAGE

(1) Surface water runoff; (2) The removal of surface water or groundwater from land by drains, grading or other means which include runoff controls to minimize erosion and sedimentation during and after construction or development, the means for preserving the water supply and the prevention or alleviation of flooding.

DRAINAGE AREA

That area in which all of the surface runoff resulting from precipitation is concentrated into a particular stream.

DRAINAGE DISTRICT

A district established by a governmental unit to build and operate facilities for drainage.

DRAINAGE SYSTEM

Pipes, swales, natural features and man-made improvements designed to carry drainage.

DRAINAGEWAY

Any natural or artificial watercourse, trench, ditch, swale or similar depression into which surface water flows.

69

 **DREDGE AND FILL**

A process which creates land by dredging material from the bottom of a body of water and depositing this material on land usually adjacent to the water.

 **DREDGING**

A method for deepening streams, swamps or coastal waters by removing solids from the bottom.

Comment: Dredging and filling can disturb natural ecological cycles. For example, dredging can destroy shell fish beds and other aquatic life; filling can destroy the feeding and breeding grounds for many fish species.

DRIVE-IN RESTAURANT

A building or portion thereof where food and/or beverages are sold in a form ready for consumption and where all or a significant portion of the consumption takes place or is designed to take place outside the confines of the building, often in a motor vehicle on the site.

Comment: Many municipalities banned drive-in restaurants because of their nuisance characteristics: litter, glare, noise, hangouts, and garish architecture. Most newer drive-ins have managed to control these adverse impacts and now differ little from conventional eating establishments.

DRIVE-IN THEATER

See THEATER, DRIVE-IN.

DRIVE-IN USE

An establishment which by design, physical facilities, service, or by packaging procedures encourages or permits customers to receive services, obtain goods, or be entertained while remaining in their motor vehicles.

DRIVEWAY

A private roadway providing access for vehicles to a parking space, garage, dwelling or other structure.

DRUG STORE

A store where the primary business is the filling of medical prescriptions and the sale of drugs, medical devices and supplies, and nonprescription medicines but where nonmedical products are sold as well.

Comment: A drug store may be distinguished from a pharmacy which deals solely with preparing and dispensing drugs and medicines. The nonmedical related products may be cards, candy, cosmetics, etc. *See* PHARMACY.

70

 **DRYWELL**

A covered pit with open jointed lining through which water from roofs, basement floors or areaways may seep or leech into the surrounding soil.

DUMP

A land site used primarily for the disposal by dumping, burial, burning or other means and for whatever purposes, of garbage, sewage, trash, refuse, junk, discarded machinery, vehicles or parts thereof, and other waste, scrap or discarded material of any kind.

DUPLEX

See DWELLING, TWO-FAMILY.

DWELLING

A structure or portion thereof which is used exclusively for human habitation.

DWELLING, ATTACHED

A one-family dwelling attached to two or more one-family dwellings by common vertical walls.

DWELLING, DETACHED

A dwelling which is not attached to any other dwelling by any means. *See Figure 5.*

Comment: The detached dwelling does not have any roof, wall or floor in common with any other dwelling unit.

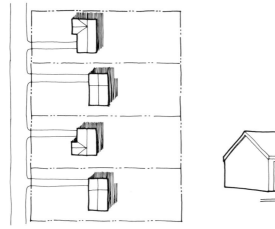

DWELLING, SINGLE FAMILY

Figure 5

71

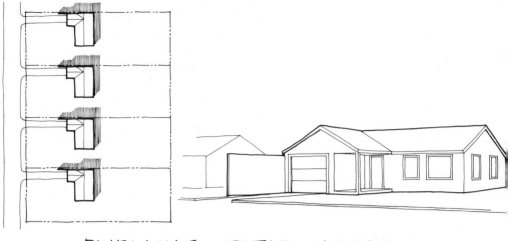

DWELLING, PATIO HOUSE

Figure 6

DWELLING,
GARDEN
APARTMENT

See DWELLING, MULTIFAMILY.

Comment: A garden apartment dwelling is actually a multifamily dwelling. The development controls would define the commonly accepted configuration of a garden apartment in terms of density (usually 10- to 15-dwelling units per acre in a suburban community, somewhat higher in an urban area and lower in a rural area), height (usually not more than a maximum of 2½ stories or 35 feet with two levels of dwelling units), and maximum length of a structure (usually between 150-200 feet). Access is usually from a common hall, although individual entrances can be provided. Dwelling units can be located on top of each other, and communities may opt to permit or prohibit the back-to-back type of units. *See Figure 10.*

DWELLING,
HIGH-RISE

An apartment building of eight or more stories. *See Figure 12.*

DWELLING,
MID-RISE

An apartment building containing from three to seven stories. *See Figure 11.*

DWELLING,
MULTIFAMILY

A dwelling containing more than two dwelling units.

72

DWELLING, PATIO HOUSE

A one-family dwelling on a separate lot with open space setbacks on three sides and with a court. *See Figure 6.*

Comment: Patio homes may be attached to similar houses on adjacent lots and still meet this definition. Also known as zero lot line homes.

DWELLING, QUADRUPLEX

Four attached dwellings in one structure in which each unit has two open space exposures and shares one or two walls with adjoining unit or units. *See Figure 8.*

DWELLING, SEMIDETACHED

A one-family dwelling attached to one other one-family dwelling by a common vertical wall, and each dwelling located on a separate lot. *See Figure 7.*

Comment: The semidetached dwelling is part of a two-family structure with the dwelling units side-by-side as opposed to one on top of the other. The semidetached dwelling also could be the end unit of a townhouse row, a patio house and a duplex.

DWELLING, SINGLE-FAMILY

A building containing one dwelling unit.

DWELLING, SINGLE-FAMILY DETACHED

A dwelling which is designed for and occupied by not more than one family and surrounded by open space or yards and which is not attached to any other dwelling by any means. *See* DWELLING, DETACHED. *See Figure 5.*

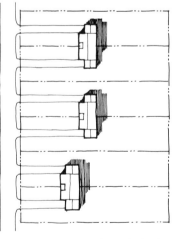

DWELLING, SEMIDETACHED

Figure 7

73

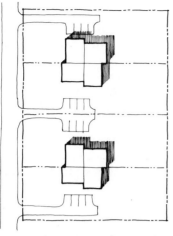

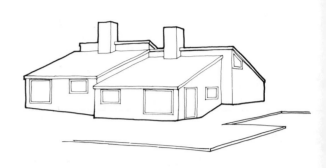

DWELLING, QUADRUPLEX

Figure 8

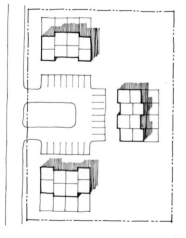

**DWELLING,
TOWNHOUSE**

A one-family dwelling in a row of at least three such units in which each unit has its own front and rear access to the outside, no unit is located over another unit, and each unit is separated from any other unit by one or more common fire resistant walls. *See Figure 9.*

Comment: Townhouses usually have separate utilities such as individual hot water and heating systems, separate electric meters, etc. However, in some condominium situations, the condominium association may arrange for bulk purchase of certain utilities and distribute it to individual dwelling units. Consequently, the definition normally would not contain a requirement for separate utility systems.

DWELLING, TOWNHOUSE

Figure 9

DWELLING, GARDEN APARTMENT
Figure 10

 **DWELLING,
TRIPLEX**

A dwelling containing three dwelling units, each of which has direct access to the outside or to a common hall.

**DWELLING,
TWO-FAMILY**

A structure on a single lot containing two dwelling units, each of which is totally separated from the other by an unpierced wall extending from ground to roof or an unpierced ceiling and floor extending from exterior wall to exterior wall, except for a common stairwell exterior to both dwelling units.

Comment: Note that this definition includes the duplex dwelling.

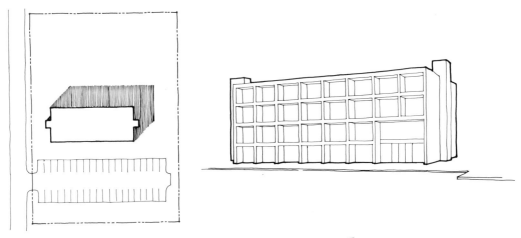

DWELLING, MID-RISE
Figure 11

DWELLING UNIT

One or more rooms, designed, occupied or intended for occupancy as separate living quarters, with cooking, sleeping and sanitary facilities provided within the dwelling unit for the exclusive use of a single family maintaining a household. *See* HOUSING UNIT.

  DWELLING UNIT, EFFICIENCY

A dwelling unit consisting of not more than one habitable room together with kitchen or kitchenette and sanitary facilities.

DYSTROPHIC LAKES

Lakes between eutrophic and swamp stages of aging.

Comment: Such lakes are shallow and have high humus content, low nutrient availability and high BOD. Such lakes are heavily stained and are commonly referred to as "brown-water lakes."

E

 **EASEMENT**

A grant of one or more of the property rights by the property owner to and/or for the use by the public, a corporation or another person or entity. *See Figure 22.*

Comment: Where property owners are reluctant to donate land for road widening purposes, an easement may be an acceptable alternative. It keeps title with the property owners, but permits the road to be widened.

 **EASEMENT, AFFIRMATIVE**

An easement which gives the holder a right to make some limited use of land owned by another. *See* EASEMENT IN GROSS.

 **EASEMENT APPURTENANT**

An easement that runs with the land.

 EASEMENT, AVIATION

An air rights easement which protects air lanes around airports.

EASEMENT, CONSERVATION

An easement precluding future or additional development of the land.

Comment: Conservation easements usually are used for the preservation of open space or a scenic view but can also be used to preserve the facade of a building.

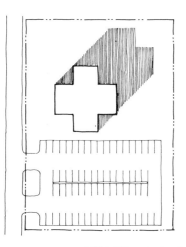 

DWELLING, HIGH-RISE

Figure 12

EASEMENT, CONTINUING	An easement that is self-perpetuating and runs with the land.
EASEMENT, DRAINAGE	An easement required for the installation of storm water sewers or drainage ditches, and/or required for the preservation or maintenance of a natural stream or water course or other drainage facility.
EASEMENT, EXPRESS	An easement that is expressly created by a deed or other instrument.
EASEMENT IN GROSS	An easement created for the personal benefit of the holder.

Comment: An easement in gross allows a person, corporation or the public to use another's land; for example, for railroad purposes or powerlines. Hagman notes (*Urban Planning and Land Development Control Law*), that the benefit of an easement in gross does not pass with the land automatically, and there's a question as to whether such easements may be assigned. The burden of an easement in gross passes with the land to all takers. *See* EASEMENT, AFFIRMATIVE.

77

 **EASEMENT, NEGATIVE**

An easement which precludes the owner of the land from doing that which the owner would be entitled to do if the easement did not exist.

Comment: Negative easements historically have been limited to easements for light, air and view.

EATING AND DRINKING PLACES

Retail establishments selling food and drink for consumption on the premises, including lunch counters and refreshment stands selling prepared foods and drinks for immediate consumption.

Comment: Restaurants, lunch counters and drinking places operated as a subordinate service facility in other establishments, such as the cafeteria of a large company, are not included in this category.

EAVE

The projecting lower edges of a roof overhanging the wall of a building.

ECOLOGICAL IMPACT

The total effect of an environmental change, either natural or man-made, on the ecology of the area.

ECOLOGY

The interrelationship of living things to one another and to their environment or the study of such relationships.

ECONOMETRICS

Statistical analysis and techniques applied to economic information and used for modeling and projection.

ECONOMIC BASE

The production, distribution and consumption of goods and services within a planning area.

Comment: Economic base, as used in planning, is commonly thought of as the sum of all activities that result in incomes for the area's inhabitants. The definition, however, is significantly broad to include all geographic and functional elements which may have an impact on the planning area, although not physically part of the area.

ECOSYSTEM

The interacting system of a biological community and its nonliving environment.

Comment: An ecosystem can be the entire biosphere, an ocean, a parcel of land, or an aquarium, depending on the context of use.

| | EDUCATIONAL INSTITUTION | A college or university authorized by the state to award degrees. |

Comment: The term as defined is applicable only to colleges and universities. Elementary, middle and high schools are defined under schools. The development ordinance must consider the fact that colleges and universities are actually mini-cities with problems relating to circulation, services, utilities, mixed uses, and peak impacts for special events such as athletics. The educational institution, with its increased demand for goods and services by the students and faculty, also imposes a severe impact on surrounding areas.

EFFICIENCY UNIT

See DWELLING UNIT, EFFICIENCY.

EFFLUENT

A discharge of pollutants, with or without treatment, into the environment.

Comment: The term is generally used to describe discharges into water.

EGRESS

An exit.

ELEEMOSYNARY or PHILANTHROPIC INSTITUTION

A private or nonprivate organization which is not organized or operated for the purpose of carrying on a trade or business and no part of the net earnings of which are for the benefit of any individual.

ELEVATION

(1) A vertical distance above or below a fixed reference level; (2) A flat scale drawing of the front, rear, or side of a building.

EMBANKMENT

An elevated man-made or natural deposit of soil, rock or other materials.

EMINENT DOMAIN

The authority of a government to take, or to authorize the taking of, private property for public use.

Comment: The U.S. Constitution Fifth Amendment requires just compensation for any taking and implicitly prohibits the taking of the private property for private use unless declared blighted.

EMISSION

A discharge of pollutants into the air.

79

 **EMISSION FACTOR**

The average amount of a pollutant emitted from each type of polluting source in relation to a specific amount of material processed.

Comment: The emission factor is used in establishing a performance standard. For example, an emission factor for a blast furnace (used to make iron) would be a number of pounds of particulates per ton of raw materials.

 **EMISSION INVENTORY**

The list of air pollutants emitted into a community's atmosphere, in amounts (usually tons) per day, by type of source.

Comment: The emission inventory is basic to the establishment of emission standards. A community may require an applicant to establish the inventory or ambient level as a basis for determining the maximum permissible level.

EMISSION STANDARD

The maximum amount of a pollutant legally permitted to be discharged from a single source, either mobile or stationary.

ENABLING ACT

The legislative act authorizing a governmental agency to do something which previously could not be done.

ENCROACHMENT

Any obstruction in a delineated floodway, right-of-way or adjacent land. *See Figure 15.*

ENLARGEMENT

An increase in the size of an existing structure.

ENRICHMENT

The addition of nitrogen, phosphorus and carbon compounds or other nutrients into a lake or other waterway.

Comment: Enrichment greatly increases the growth potential for algae and aquatic plants. Most frequently, enrichment results from the inflow of sewage effluent or from fertilizer runoff.

ENVIRONMENT

The sum of all external conditions and influences affecting the life, development and, ultimately, the survival of an organism.

ENVIRONMENTAL IMPACT STATEMENT (EIS)

A statement on the effect of development proposals and other major actions which significantly affect the environment.

Comment: The environmental impact statement provides the information needed to evaluate the effects of a proposed project upon the environment. The statement usually consists of an inventory of existing environmental conditions at the project site and in the surrounding region. The inventory includes air, water quality, water supply, hydrology, geology, soil, topography, vegetation, wildlife, aquatic organisms, ecology, demography, land use, aesthetics, history and archaeology. The EIS also includes a project description and a list of all licenses, permits or other approvals required by law. The environmental impact statement assesses the probable impact of the project upon all the inventory items and includes a listing of adverse environmental impacts that cannot be avoided. The statement also includes what steps the applicant proposes to take to minimize adverse environmental impacts during construction and operation and whether there are alternatives to any part of the project.

 ENVIRONMENTALLY SENSITIVE AREA

See CRITICAL AREA.

 **EROSION**

The detachment and movement of soil or rock fragments, or the wearing away of the land surface by water, wind, ice and gravity.

 ESSENTIAL SERVICES

The erection, construction, alteration, or maintenance of underground, surface or overhead electrical, gas, steam, water and sewerage transmission and collection systems and the equipment and appurtenances necessary for such systems to furnish an adequate level of public service.

ESTABLISHMENT

An economic unit, generally at a single physical location, where business is conducted or services or industrial operations performed.

 **ESTUARIES**

Areas where the fresh water meets salt water such as bays, mouths of rivers, salt marshes and lagoons.

 **EUTROPHIC LAKES**

Shallow lakes, weed-choked at the edges and very rich in nutrients.

Comment: Eutrophic lakes are characterized by large amounts of algae, low water transparency, low dissolved oxygen and high BOD.

 **EUTROPHICATION**

The normally slow aging process by which a lake evolves into a bog or marsh and ultimately assumes a completely terrestrial state and disappears.

EVALUATION

A process to measure the success of an activity and how closely the results meet the anticipated outcome defined as part of the initial phase of the activity.

EVAPORATION PONDS

Shallow, artificial ponds where sewage sludge is pumped, permitted to dry and either removed or buried by more sludge.

EXCAVATION

Removal or recovery by any means whatsoever of soil, rock, minerals, mineral substances or organic substances other than vegetation, from water or land on or beneath the surface thereof, or beneath the land surface, whether exposed or submerged.

EXCLUSIONARY ZONING

Development regulations which result in the exclusion of low- and moderate-income and minority families from a community.

EXCLUSIVE USE DISTRICT

A zoning district that allows only one use or a limited range of sensitive uses.

EXISTING GRADE or ELEVATION

The vertical location of the ground surface prior to excavating or filling.

EXISTING USE

The use of a lot or structure at the time of the enactment of a zoning ordinance.

Comment: Most municipalities, at the time a new zoning or development ordinance is proposed, will attempt to survey existing uses in order to provide an accurate record of pre-existing nonconforming uses. The pre-existing nonconforming use, legal at the time of the passage of the ordinance but made nonconforming as a result of the ordinance, has a legal right to continue. Future problems arise because of confusion as to the extent and nature of the uses at the time of passage. Hence, an inventory is often necessary to insure that non-conforming uses do not expand illegally.

EXIT RAMP, ENTRANCE RAMP

Access lanes leading to and from a limited access highway.

| **EXTENDED CARE FACILITY** | A long-term care facility or a distinct part of a facility licensed or approved as a nursing home, infirmary unit of a home for the aged or a governmental medical institution. *See* LONG-TERM CARE FACILITY and NURSING HOME. |

EXTENSION

An increase in the amount of existing floor area within an existing building.

EXTERIOR WALL

Any wall which defines the exterior boundaries of a building or structure.

F

FABRICATION AND ASSEMBLY

The manufacturing from standardized parts of a distinct object differing from the individual components.

Comment: The term fabrication and assembly often is used to describe a general class of permitted uses. It usually involves materials with form and substance (as opposed to liquid or gas) with a physical, as opposed to chemical, mating or joining of the individual parts.

FACADE

The exterior wall of a building exposed to public view or that wall viewed by persons not within the building. *See Figure 13.*

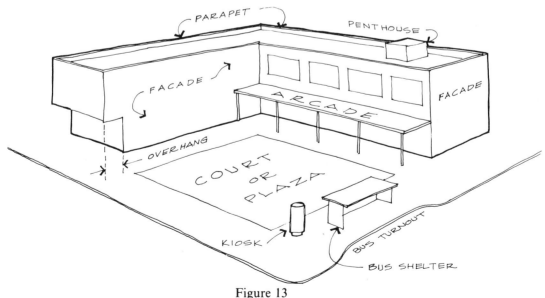

Figure 13

83

▨	**FACTORY**	A building in which semifinished or finished materials are converted to a different form or state or where goods are manufactured, assembled, treated, or processed.
▨	**FACTORY-BUILT HOUSE**	A dwelling unit that is constructed and assembled at a factory and transported to the building's site and placed on a prebuilt foundation.
▨ ▧	**FAIR MARKET VALUE**	The price of a building or land which would be agreed upon voluntarily in fair negotiations between a knowledgable owner willing, but not forced, to sell and a knowledgable buyer willing, but not forced, to buy.

Comment: The definition describes an ideal abstract situation. In real life situations, brokers use a variety of methods to establish the fair market value including comparable sales, income capitalization and replacement value.

▨	**FAIR SHARE HOUSING PLANS**	Plans designed to promote low- and moderate-income housing opportunities equitably distributed among all of a region's communities.
▲	**FALLOW LAND**	Farmland left uncultivated.
▨	**FAMILY**	One or more individuals occupying a dwelling unit and living as a single household unit.

Comment: The above definition places no limit on the number of unrelated individuals that may occupy the dwelling unit. Up to very recently, definitions of family usually limited the number of unrelated individuals, often as low as three or four. Thus, under the old definition a family was frequently defined as "one or more persons related by blood, marriage, adoption or guardianship, and not more than three persons not so related."

The change to unlimited numbers of unrelated individuals reflects the most recent decision by the New Jersey Supreme Court (*State* v. *Baker,* N.J. Supreme Court, A-59), decided July 30, 1979. In this case, the Court threw out a Plainfield, New Jersey, ordinance that established a limit on the number of unrelated individuals. It suggested that by limiting unrelated individuals it prohibited many reasonable occupancies such as unrelated widows, bachelors, or "even judges." The decision suggested that the municipality could regulate density by limiting the number of occupants in relation to the number of bedrooms, bathrooms, or a minimum number of square feet per occupant. It also suggested that traffic could be restricted by limiting the number of vehicles.

The New Jersey decision was decided upon New Jersey State Constitutional grounds which were interpreted more restrictively than the Federal Constitution. The leading federal case is *Village of Belle Terre* v. *Boraas* 416 *U.S.* 1, 9, *9L.Ed.* 2d 797 (1974) in which the U.S. Supreme Court upheld limits on the occupancy of unrelated individuals. *See* GROUP FAMILY HOUSEHOLD.

FARM or FARMLAND   A parcel of land used for agricultural activities.

Comment: Many states have minimum acreage and/or income production requirements for a "farm" classification. In New Jersey the minimum requirement to qualify for a reduced tax assessment is five acres and gross revenues of $500 per year.

FARM STAND   A booth or stall located on a farm from which produce and farm products are sold to the general public.

Comment: Very often municipalities impose the additional restriction that the farm products sold at the booth or stall must be raised on the farm or the land upon which the booth or stall is located. In actual practice, this has proved to be impractical. A better approach is to place restrictions on the size of the stand in terms of the availability of parking and size of the lot.

FARM STRUCTURE   Any building or structure used for agricultural purposes.

FAST-FOOD RESTAURANT   An establishment whose principal business is the sale of pre-prepared or rapidly prepared food directly to the customer in a ready-to-consume state for consumption either within the restaurant building or off premises.

Comment: The distinction between the fast-food restaurant and other types of restaurants is rapidly becoming blurred. The major objection to fast-food restaurants came from the adverse impacts including high traffic, glare, garish design, litter and noise. Often they became hangouts. With stringent performance standards these problems can be controlled and there appears to be little reason to differentiate between fast-food restaurants and other types of restaurants. *See* DRIVE-IN RESTAURANT.

85

 **FAULT AREA**

Areas of land along a break or fracture in rock strata that may become dislocated along the line of fracture.

Comment: Buildings in a fault area are more likely to suffer damage when there are earthquakes or tremors along the fault. In addition, waste disposal from residential or industrial uses locating over fault areas can adversely affect groundwater supply.

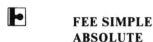 **FEASIBILITY STUDY**

An analysis of a specific project or program to determine if it can be successfully carried out.

 **FEE SIMPLE ABSOLUTE**

The most complete set of private property land rights, including mineral rights below the surface, surface rights, and air rights.

FEEDLOT

A relatively small, confined land area for fattening cattle or holding temporarily for shipment.

 **FEN**

A low-lying land area partly covered by water.

FENCE

An artificially constructed barrier of any material or combination of materials erected to enclose or screen areas of land.

Comment: Development regulations should include provisions for fences. Generally, they should be divided into categories of open, semi-open and closed fences and regulations should establish maximum heights and setbacks for the different categories. For example, an open fence, such as a split rail fence, might be permitted anywhere on a particular lot. Closed fences such as brick might be restricted to a maximum height of six feet and be required to meet all setback requirements for principal structures in the zone.

 **FILL**

Sand, gravel, earth or other materials of any composition whatsoever placed or deposited by humans. *See Figure 21.*

FILLING

The process of depositing fill in low-lying marshy or water areas to create usable land. *See* LAND RECLAMATION and MADE LAND.

FILLING STATION

See AUTOMOBILE SERVICE STATION.

FILTRATION

In waste water treatment, the mechanical process that removes particulate matter from water, usually by passing it through sand.

 **FINAL APPROVAL**

The last official action of the planning board or board of adjustment taken on a development plan which has been given preliminary approval, after all conditions and requirements have been met, and the required improvements have been installed or guarantees properly posted for their installation, or approval conditioned upon the posting of such guarantees.

 **FINAL PLAN**

See PLAT, FINAL.

FINANCE, INSURANCE AND REAL ESTATE

Establishments such as, but not limited to, banks and trust companies, credit agencies, investment companies, brokers and dealers of securities and commodities, security and commodity exchanges, insurance agents, brokers, lessors, lessees, buyers, sellers, agents and developers of real estate.

FINGER FILL CANALS

Waterfront residential developments created by the dredging and filling of shallow bays and estuaries, built on fingerlike projections of land interspersed with deep, narrow canals.

FINISH ELEVATION

The proposed elevation of the land surface of a site after completion of all site preparation work. *See* GRADE, FINISHED.

FINISHED PRODUCT

The end result of a manufacturing process which is ready for utilization or consumption by the ultimate consumer.

Comment: The above definition, from the *Standard Industrial Classification Manual,* should be read in conjunction with the definition and comments of "semi-finished product" in this volume.

FISH FARM

An area devoted to the cultivation of fish and other seafood for commercial sale.

FISHING, HUNTING, TRAPPING

Establishments primarily engaged in commercial fishing, including shell fish marine products, operating fish hatcheries and fish and game preserves, and the killing of animals by gunning or the capture in mechanical or other types of devices for commercial gain.

FLAG LOT

A lot not fronting on or abutting a public road and where access to the public road is by a narrow, private right-of-way. *See Figure 18.*

Comment: Flag lots are permitted in rural and developing municipalities to permit development of backland areas while still maintaining their rural character. The usual requirements for a flag lot are as follows: minimum lot area at least twice the area in the zone where located exclusive of the right-of-way connecting the lot with the public road; minimum front, side and rear yard requirements to be met on the portion excluding the right-of-way; minimum of 20 feet and maximum of 50 feet for right-of-way; not more than one flag lot for each right-of-way; rights-of-way should be a minimum distance apart of at least the minimum lot width in the particular zone.

FLEA MARKET

An occasional or periodic market held in an open area or structure where groups of individual sellers offer goods for sale to the public.

Comment: Flea markets often are regularly scheduled, i.e., weekends and holidays, and while most are held outdoors or under sheds, a recent trend is to utilize large, previously vacant buildings such as discount stores or vacant shopping centers. The key consideration is that there are no long-term leases between the sellers and operators and that often the sellers use their own vehicles for display or set up temporary tables for their wares. For zoning purposes, they should be considered as temporary uses subject to site plan review to insure adequate circulation, safety and off-street parking.

FLOATING ZONE

An unmapped zoning district where all the zone requirements are contained in the ordinance and the zone is fixed on the map only when an application for development, meeting the zone requirements, is approved.

Comment: Floating zones generally have declined in popularity because of charges they closely resemble spot zoning and contract zoning, both illegal under current case law. The most appropriate application appears to be in rural communities where large tracts of land may be developed in accordance with planned development regulations providing the ordinance requirements are met for conversion of the land from the previous rural designation to a development zone. Some of these ordinance regulations might include direct access to major roads, availability of public water and public sewer, proximity to other municipal facilities and services, etc.

FLOCCULATION

In waste water treatment, the process of separating suspended solids by chemical creation of clumps or flocs.

FLOOD

The temporary overflowing of water onto land which is usually devoid of surface water.

FLOOD, BASE FLOOD ELEVATION

See BASE FLOOD ELEVATION.

FLOOD DAMAGE POTENTIAL

The susceptibility of a specific land use at a particular location to damage by flooding, and the potential of the specific land use to increase off-site flooding or flood-related damages.

FLOOD FRINGE AREA

That portion of the flood hazard area outside of the floodway based on the total area inundated during the regulatory base flood plus twenty-five percent of the regulatory base flood discharge. *See* FLOODWAY; FLOOD, REGULATORY BASE and FLOOD, REGULATORY BASE FLOOD DISCHARGE. *See Figure 15.*

FLOOD HAZARD AREA

The flood plain consisting of the floodway and the flood fringe area. *See* FLOOD PLAIN. *See Figure 15.*

FLOOD HAZARD DESIGN ELEVATION

The highest elevation, expressed in feet above sea level, of the level of floodwaters which delineates the flood fringe area.

FLOOD INSURANCE RATE MAP

The official map on which the Federal Insurance Administration has delineated both the areas of special flood hazards and the risk premium zones applicable to the community.

FLOOD OF RECORD

A flood which has occurred for which there are accurate local records available.

FLOOD, REGULATORY BASE

Flood having a one percent chance of being equalled or exceeded in any given year.

Comment: This is often referred to as a 100-year flood.

 **FLOOD,
REGULATORY BASE
FLOOD DISCHARGE**

The rate of flow produced by the regulatory base flood measured in cubic feet per second.

 **FLOOD PLAIN**

The channel and the relatively flat area adjoining the channel of a natural stream or river which has been or may be covered by floodwater. *See Figure 15.*

 **FLOODPROOFING**

A combination of structural provisions, changes or adjustments to properties and structures subject to flooding for the reduction or elimination of flood damage to properties, water and sanitary facilities and other utilities, structures and the contents of buildings.

 **FLOODWAY**

The channel of a natural stream or river and portions of the flood plain adjoining the channel, which are reasonably required to carry and discharge the floodwater or flood flow of any natural stream or river. *See* FLOODWAY, REGULATORY. *See Figure 15.*

 **FLOODWAY,
REGULATORY**

The channel and the adjacent land areas that must be reserved in order to discharge the regulatory base flood without cumulatively increasing the water surface elevation more than two tenths of one foot.

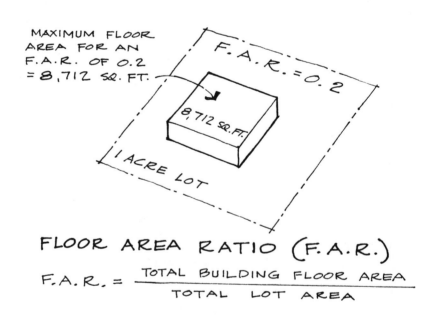

Figure 14

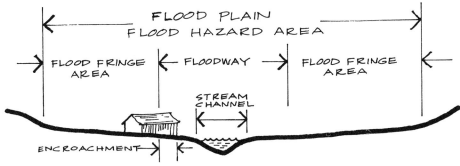

FLOOD PLAIN CROSS SECTION

Figure 15

FLOOR AREA, GROSS

The sum of the gross horizontal areas of the several floors of a building measured from the exterior face of exterior walls, or from the centerline of a wall separating two buildings, but not including interior parking spaces, loading space for motor vehicles, or any space where the floor-to-ceiling height is less than six feet.

Comment: Interior parking spaces and loading spaces are excluded in order not to penalize applicants that include these facilities.

FLOOR AREA, NET

The total of all floor areas of a building, excluding stairwells and elevator shafts, equipment rooms, interior vehicular parking or loading; and all floors below the first or ground floor, except when used or intended to be used for human habitation or service to the public.

Comment: Very often, for ease of administration, net floor area is expressed as gross floor area minus a certain percentage. Empirically, stairwells, elevator shafts, equipment room and utility rooms generally average out to about 15% of the gross floor area. Thus, net floor area may be defined as gross floor area minus 15%.

FLOOR AREA RATIO

The gross floor area of all buildings on a lot divided by the lot area. *See Figure 14.*

FLORICULTURE

The cultivation of ornamental flowering plants.

FLOWMETER

In waste water treatment, a meter that indicates the rate at which waste water flows.

FLUE GAS

A mixture of gases resulting from combustion which emerges from a chimney.

91

FLUME — A man-made channel, which carries water.

FLY ASH — All partially incinerated solids that are carried in a gas stream.

FLY-IN DEVELOPMENT — A residential development planned and integrated with airport facilities and directly accessible to recreational flyers.

FOOD PROCESSING ESTABLISHMENT — A commercial establishment in which food is processed or otherwise prepared for human consumption but not consumed on the premises.

FOOTCANDLE — The unit of illumination when the foot is the unit of length.

Comment: The footcandle is the illumination on a surface one square foot in area on which there is a uniformly distributed flux of one lumen. One footcandle equals one lumen per square foot. In zoning ordinances, the standard for various light sources is established in footcandles. *See* CANDLEPOWER.

FOREST — Areas or stands of trees the majority of which are greater than 12 inches caliper measured four feet above grade, covering an area greater than one-quarter acre; or groves of mature trees without regard to minimum area consisting of more than ten individual specimens.

FORESTRY — Establishments primarily engaged in the operation of timber tracts, tree farms, forest nurseries, the gathering of forest products, or in performing forest services.

FORMATION — A geologic bed or consecutive series of beds sufficiently homogeneous or distinctive to be a unit.

FOSSIL FUELS — Coals, oil and animal gas; so called because they are derived from the remains of ancient plant and animal life.

FRATERNAL ORGANIZATION — A group of people formally organized for a common interest, usually cultural, religious or entertainment, with regular meetings, rituals and formal written membership requirements.

Comment: Examples of such groups are Masons or the Knights of Columbus. The clubhouses usually were located in residential neighborhoods, but newer ordinances have properly located them in business areas because they usually draw their membership from a wide geographic area. In addition, the club facilities often are used for weddings, bingo and weekend catering and can become nuisances to surrounding residences. *See* CLUB and MEMBERSHIP ORGANIZATION.

FRATERNITY HOUSE A dwelling or dwelling unit maintained exclusively for fraternity members and their guests or visitors and affiliated with an academic or professional college, university or other institution of higher learning.

Comment: Unless a community has a separate educational zone, fraternity and sorority houses usually are permitted as conditional uses in appropriate zones.

FREEWAY *See* STREET, FREEWAY.

FREIGHT FORWARDING Establishments primarily engaged in undertaking the transportation of goods from shippers to receivers for a charge covering the entire transporation route, and in turn, making use of the services of other transportation establishments as instrumentalities in effecting delivery.

FRONTAGE That side of a lot abutting on a street; the front lot line. *See Figure 20.*

Comment: On corner or through lots the frontage may be designated by the owner but it should be consistent with the orientation of the other lots and improvements on the same side of the street. On improved lots the frontage is usually the side where the main building entrance is located and in the general direction in which the principal building faces.

FRONT FOOT A measure of land width, being one foot along the front lot line of a property.

FRONT LOT LINE *See* LOT LINE, FRONT.

FRONT YARD *See* YARD, FRONT.

FUNERAL HOME A building used for the preparation of the deceased for burial and the display of the deceased and ceremonies connected therewith before burial or cremation.

Comment: Funeral homes are generally very stable types of uses and are extremely well maintained. The only

93

potential problem is the necessity for adequate off-street parking and stacking room for cars lined up for the funeral procession.

G

GAME or GAMBLING GAME — Any banking or percentage game played with cards, dice or any mechanical device or machine for money, property or any representative of value, and located exclusively within a casino.

GAMING or GAMBLING — The dealing, operating, carrying on, conducting, maintaining or exposing for pay of any game.

GAMING or GAMBLING ESTABLISHMENT — Any premises wherein or whereon gaming is done.

GAMING DEVICE or GAMING EQUIPMENT — Any mechanical contrivance or machine used in connection with gaming or any game.

GARAGE — A deck, building or structure, or part thereof, used or intended to be used for the parking and storage of vehicles.

GARAGE, COMMUNITY — A garage used exclusively for the parking and storage of vehicles owned or operated by residents of nearby dwelling units and their guests, which is not operated as a commercial enterprise and is not available to the general public, and which is owned, leased or cooperatively operated by such residents.

GARAGE, MUNICIPAL — A structure owned or operated by a municipality and used primarily for the parking and storing of vehicles owned by the general public.

GARAGE, PRIVATE CUSTOMER AND EMPLOYEE — A structure which is accessory to a nonretail commercial or manufacturing establishment, building or use and is primarily for the parking and storage of vehicles operated by the customers, visitors and employees of such building, and which is not available to the general public.

94

GARAGE, PRIVATE RESIDENTIAL	A structure which is accessory to a residential building and which is used for the parking and storage of vehicles owned and operated by the residents thereof, and which is not a separate commercial enterprise available to the general public.

GARAGE, PRIVATE RESIDENTIAL

A structure which is accessory to a residential building and which is used for the parking and storage of vehicles owned and operated by the residents thereof, and which is not a separate commercial enterprise available to the general public.

GARAGE, PUBLIC

A building, or portion thereof, other than a private customer and employee garage or private residential garage, used primarily for the parking and storage of vehicles and available to the general public.

GARAGE, REPAIR

Any building, premises and land in which or upon which a business, service or industry involving the maintenance, servicing, repair or painting of vehicles is conducted or rendered. *See* AUTOMOTIVE REPAIR, SERVICES AND GARAGES.

GARBAGE

Animal and vegetable waste resulting from the handling, storage, sale, preparation, cooking and serving of foods. *See* SOLID WASTE.

GARDEN APARTMENT

See DWELLING, MULTIFAMILY.

GASOLINE STATION

See AUTOMOBILE SERVICE STATION.

GENERAL PUBLIC

Any and all individuals without any prior qualifications.

Comment: Facilities open to the general public may charge fees for admission or payment for services.

GLARE

The effect produced by brightness sufficient to cause annoyance, discomfort, or loss in visual performance and visibility.

Comment: The definition is subjective but can be applied in a given situation by establishing a reference line (usually the lot or zone line) and maximum footcandle reading.

GOLF COURSE

A tract of land for playing golf, improved with tees, greens, fairways, hazards, and which may include clubhouses and shelters. *See* COUNTRY CLUB.

GOVERNMENT AGENCY

Any department, commission, independent agency or instrumentality of the United States, of a state, county, incorporated or unincorporated municipality, township, authority, district or other governmental unit.

95

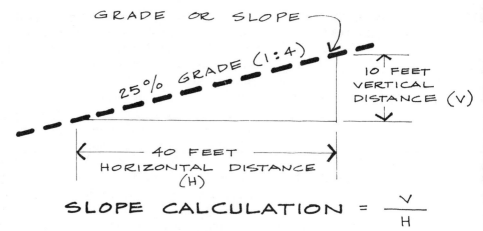

SLOPE CALCULATION = $\dfrac{V}{H}$

Figure 16

 **GRADE**

The degree of rise or descent of a sloping surface. *See Figure 16.*

 **GRADE, FINISHED**

The final elevation of the ground surface after development. *See* FINISH ELEVATION. *See Figure 21.*

 **GRADE, NATURAL**

The elevation of the ground surface in its natural state, before man-made alterations. *See* NATURAL GROUND SURFACE. *See Figure 21.*

 **GRADING**

Any stripping, cutting, filling, stockpiling of earth or land, including the land in its cut or filled condition.

GRAIN LOADING

The rate of emission of particulate matter from a polluting source.

Comment: Measurement is made in grains of particulate matter per cubic foot of gas emitted.

GRANT

(1) An instrument that conveys some estate or interest in the lands which it embraces; (2) Financial aid.

GRAPHIC SCALE

See SCALE.

GRAVEL PIT

An open land area where sand, gravel and rock fragments are mined or excavated for sale or off-tract use.

Comment: Gravel pits usually include sifting, crushing and washing as part of the primary operation. To excavate the rock, blasting also may be necessary. In addition, the land is often left in a highly erodible state incapable

96

of any reuse. Any ordinance which permits gravel pits should require a soil erosion plan and reuse plan for the land. *See* QUARRY and SAND PIT.

GREASE TRAP

A device in which the grease present in sewage is intercepted and congealed by cooling, and from which it may be skimmed of liquid wastes for disposal.

GREEN AREA

Land shown on a development plan, master plan or official map for preservation, recreation, landscaping or park.

GREENBELT

An open area which may be cultivated or maintained in a natural state surrounding development or used as a buffer between land uses or to mark the edge of an urban or developed area.

GREENHOUSE

A building whose roof and sides are made largely of glass or other transparent or translucent material and in which the temperature and humidity can be regulated for the cultivation of delicate or out-of-season plants for subsequent sale or for personal enjoyment. *See* NURSERY.

GRID SYSTEM

A map coordinated system that allows the identification of a land area by two coordinate numbers. *See Figure 24.*

GROSS FLOOR AREA

See FLOOR AREA, GROSS and NET.

GROSS HABITABLE FLOOR AREA

See FLOOR AREA, NET.

GROSS LEASABLE AREA

The total floor area for which the tenant pays rent and which is designed for the tenant's occupancy and exclusive use.

Comment: Gross leasable area does not include public or common areas such as utility rooms, stairwells, malls, etc.

GROUND COVER

Grasses or other plants grown to keep soil from being blown or washed away.

GROUND COVERAGE

See LOT COVERAGE.

GROUND FLOOR

The first floor of a building other than a cellar or basement.

97

GROUNDWATER

The supply of freshwater under the surface in an aquifer or soil that forms the natural reservoir for potable water. *See Figure 20.*

GROUNDWATER RUNOFF

Groundwater that is discharged into a stream channel as spring or seepage water.

GROUP CARE FACILITY

A facility or dwelling unit housing persons unrelated by blood or marriage and operating as a group family household.

Comment: A group care facility may include half-way houses; recovery homes; and homes for orphans, foster children, the elderly, battered children and women. It also could include a specialized treatment facility providing less than primary health care. *See* GROUP FAMILY HOUSEHOLD.

GROUP FAMILY HOUSEHOLD

A group of individuals not related by blood, marriage, adoption or guardianship living together in a dwelling unit as a single housekeeping unit under a common housekeeping management plan based on an intentionally structured relationship providing organization and stability. *See* FAMILY.

GROUP LIVING QUARTERS

See GROUP QUARTERS and DORMITORY.

GROUP QUARTERS

A dwelling that houses unrelated individuals.

Comment: Group quarters include fraternities, sororities, army barracks, dormitories and the like.

GROWTH MANAGEMENT

Techniques used by government to control the rate, amount and type of development.

H

HABITABLE FLOOR AREA

See MINIMUM-HABITABLE FLOOR AREA.

HABITABLE ROOM

Any room in a dwelling unit other than a kitchen, bathroom, closet, pantry, hallway, cellar, storage space, garage and basement recreation room.

98

HABITAT

The sum total of all the environmental factors of a specific place that is occupied by an organism, a population or a community.

HAIRPIN MARKING

A double-painted line separating parking stalls.

HALF STORY

See STORY, HALF. *See Figure 17.*

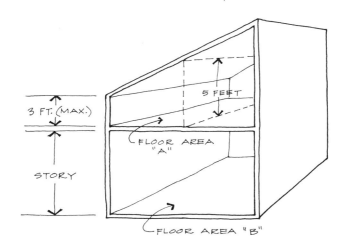

3 FT. (MAX.)

5 FEET

FLOOR AREA "A"

STORY

FLOOR AREA "B"

IF FLOOR AREA "A" IS AT LEAST 40% OF FLOOR AREA "B" — THEN "A" IS A HALF STORY.

Figure 17

HALFWAY HOUSE

See BOARDING HOME FOR SHELTERED CARE.

HAMLET

A small settlement or village.

HAMMERMILL

A broad category of high-speed equipment that uses pivoted or fixed hammers or cutters to crush, grind, chip or shred solid wastes.

HARDSHIP VARIANCE

See VARIANCE, HARDSHIP.

HAZARDOUS AIR POLLUTANT

A pollutant to which no ambient air quality standard is applicable and that may cause or contribute to an increase in mortality or serious illness.

Comment: Examples of hazardous air pollutants are asbestos, beryllium and mercury.

99

▲ HAZARDOUS MATERIAL DISPOSAL

A method for the safe disposal of hazardous materials.

▲ HAZARDOUS MATERIALS

Includes, but are not limited to, inorganic mineral acids of sulfur, flourine, chlorine, nitrogen, chromium, phosphorous, selenium and arsenic and their common salts; lead, nickle and mercury and their inorganic salts or metallo-organic derivatives; coal, tar acids such as phenol and cresols and their salts and all radioactive materials.

■ HEALTH CARE FACILITY

A facility or institution, whether public or private, principally engaged in providing services for health maintenance, diagnosis or treatment of human disease, pain, injury, deformity or physical condition, including, but not limited to, a general hospital, special hospital, mental hospital, public health center, diagnostic center, treatment center, rehabilitation center, extended care facility, skilled nursing home, nursing home, intermediate care facility, tuberculosis hospital, chronic disease hospital, maternity hospital, outpatient clinic, dispensary, home health care agency, boarding home or other home for sheltered care, and bioanalytical laboratory or central services facility serving one or more such institutions but excluding institutions that provide healing solely by prayer. *See* HEALTH SERVICES.

▲ HEALTH PLANNING

The study of the present status and future needs of the existing and probable future population for health facilities and services.

■ HEALTH SERVICES

Establishments primarily engaged in furnishing medical, surgical or other services to individuals, including the offices of physicians, dentists, and other health practitioners, medical and dental laboratories, out-patient care facilities, blood banks, and oxygen and miscellaneous types of medical supplies and services.

Comment: Hospitals are omitted from the list although obviously they are a prime supplier of health services. However, the standards required for their establishment and location are set by state and/or federal agencies and the scale of operation is considerably more intensive when compared with the other establishments. *See* HEALTH CARE FACILITY.

HEAT ISLAND EFFECT

An air circulation problem peculiar to urban areas whereby heat from buildings, structures, pavements and concentrations of pollutants create a haze dome that prevents rising hot air from being cooled at its normal rate.

HEIGHT

The vertical distance of a structure measured from the average elevation of the finished grade within 20 feet of the structure to the highest point of the structure. *See* BUILDING HEIGHT. *See Figure 3.*

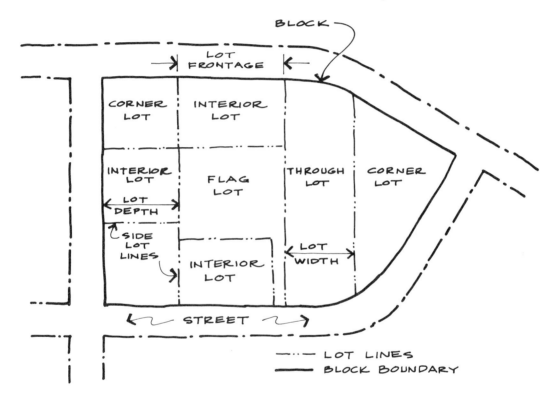

Figure 18

HELIPORT

An area, either at ground level or elevated on a structure, licensed or approved for the loading and takeoff of helicopters, and including auxiliary facilities such as parking, waiting room, fueling and maintenance equipment.

HELISTOP

A heliport, but without auxiliary facilities such as parking, waiting room, fueling and maintenance equipment.

HIGH-RISE

See DWELLING, HIGH-RISE.

| | HIGHEST AND BEST USE | An appraisal concept that determines the use of a particular property likely to produce the greatest net return in the foreseeable future. |

HIGHEST AND BEST USE

An appraisal concept that determines the use of a particular property likely to produce the greatest net return in the foreseeable future.

Comment: The term highest and best use has little validity in planning or zoning studies. Its major application is probably as a comparison between several uses to determine which is more profitable.

HIGHWAY

See STREETS.

HISTORIC AREA

A district or zone designated by a local authority, state or federal government within which the buildings, structures, appurtenances and places are of basic and vital importance because of their association with history, or because of their unique architectural style and scale, including color, proportion, form and architectural detail, or because of their being a part of or related to a square, park, or area the design or general arrangement of which should be preserved and/or developed according to a fixed plan based on cultural, historical or architectural motives or purposes.

Comment: Designation by the appropriate state agency is a prerequisite for listing by the National Register of Historic Places.

HISTORIC BUILDING

Any building or structure which is historically or architecturally significant.

HISTORIC BUILDING STYLES

Recognized architectural styles such as Colonial; Federal; Greek Revival; Victorian; Gothic Revival; Victorian Gothic; Romanesque Revival. *See Figure 19.*

Comment: The definition is actually a partial listing of major American historic building styles. For purposes of historic district zoning for a particular area, this listing might be revised as appropriate and detailed architectural definitions of each style are added.

HISTORIC DISTRICT

See HISTORIC AREA.

HISTORIC PRESERVATION

The protection, rehabilitation, and restorations of districts, sites, buildings, structures and artifacts significant in American history, architecture, archaeology, or culture.

102

COLONIAL
(1700-1720)

EARLY GEORGIAN
(1720-1760)

LATE GEORGIAN
(1760-1780)

FEDERAL
(1780-1820)

GREEK REVIVAL
(1820-1840)

VICTORIAN
(1830-1850)

HISTORIC BUILDING STYLES

Figure 19

103

HISTORIC SITE

A structure or place of outstanding historical and cultural significance and designated as such, by state or federal government.

 **HI-VOLUME (HI-VOL) SAMPLER**

A device used in the measurement and analysis of suspended particulate pollution.

 HOME OCCUPATION

Any activity carried out for gain by a resident conducted as an accessory use in the resident's dwelling unit.

Comment: The above definition is the broadest possible one covering all home occupations. It simply states that any activity which is carried out for gain by a resident in his or her dwelling unit is a home occupation. It doesn't mean that a community must permit home occupations, or that the community cannot control and limit home occupations. Controls are more properly accomplished within the body of the ordinance. In those zones where home occupations are permitted, the development ordinance also may impose reasonable restrictions, including the number of nonresident employees, if any; controls on signs, if allowed at all; the maximum amount of square footage to be used for the home occupation; and parking requirements.

The recommended definition also avoids the necessity of attempting to spell out which home occupations would be permitted. Rather, it states that *any* home occupation that meets the performance standards may be permitted. To minimize any impact from home occupations in residential zones, additional restrictions might include one specifying that no goods, chattels, materials, supplies or items of any kind can be delivered either to or from the premises in connection with the home occupation except in a passenger automobile owned by the resident. A further limitation might include prohibiting clients, patrons or customers or the retail sale of products on the premises. Obviously, this latter prohibition would rule out medical offices or professional home offices, because clients do visit these offices. In areas or zones where appropriate, these restrictions can be altered or waived. With a broad definition and performance standards, the community can determine the location, extent, and intensity of home occupations.

 HOME PROFESSIONAL OFFICE

A home occupation consisting of the office of a practitioner of a recognized profession.

Comment: The major question is what is a recognized profession? Some points worth noting is that the granting of a state license in and by itself is not an indication of a recognized profession. Customary home professional offices usually include attorneys, medical practitioners, engineers, and architects. As noted in the definition of "home occupation," the necessity to define a recognized profession can be avoided if performance standards are established for any home occupation, with the home professional office being one under that category.

HOMEOWNERS ASSOCIATION

A community association, other than a condominium association, which is organized in a development in which individual owners share common interests in open space or facilities.

Comment: The homeowners association usually holds title to certain common property, manages and maintains the common property, and enforces certain covenants and restrictions. Condominium associations differ from homeowners associations in that the condominium associations do not have title to the common property.

HORTICULTURE

The cultivation of a garden or orchard.

HOSPITAL

An institution providing primary health services and medical or surgical care to persons, primarily inpatients, suffering from illness, disease, injury, deformity and other abnormal physical or mental conditions, and including, as an integral part of the institution, related facilities such as laboratories, outpatient facilities or training facilities.

HOTEL

A facility offering transient lodging accommodations to the general public and providing additional services such as restaurants, meeting rooms, and recreation facilities. *See* BOARDING HOUSE; INN; MOTEL; RESORT and TOURIST HOME.

HOUSE TRAILER

See MOBILE HOME.

HOUSEHOLD

A family living together in a single dwelling unit, with common access to, and common use of, all living and eating areas and all areas and facilities for the preparation and storage of food within the dwelling unit.

105

**HOUSING
ASSISTANCE
PLAN (HAP)**

The identification of housing needs and the establishment of housing goals for low- and moderate-income households as developed by applicants for community development block grants under the requirements of the U.S. Department of Housing and Urban Development.

**HOUSING FOR THE
ELDERLY**

Multifamily housing designed for older people.

Comment: Such housing usually has wider doors, elevators that can accommodate wheelchairs, special support and hand bars, and bathroom and kitchen facilities designed specifically for the elderly. It also may include care facilities, central recreation areas, and accessory medical facilities. Elderly person housing may be private or subsidized under one or more governmental programs. The definition of elderly is usually 62 years of age or older for federally assisted projects.

HOUSING REGION

That geographic area, surrounding or adjacent to a municipality, from which the bulk of the employment within the municipality is drawn; or the area surrounding or adjacent to the municipality where most of the residents of the municipality are employed.

Comment: The question of housing region has assumed even greater importance in the past several years because of its application in exclusionary housing cases. In the *Mt. Laurel* Case (*Southern Burlington County NAACP* v. *Township of Mt. Laurel,* 67 NJ 151, 1975), the Court determined the Mt. Laurel housing region as a 20-mile radius from Camden but stopping at the State boundary. Norman Williams, in *After Mt. Laurel: The New Suburban Zoning,* edited by Rose and Rothman, 1977, defined the housing region as "the area of continuous settlement which coincides roughly with the area within which substantial numbers of people commute to work in the old center." Williams uses the phrase, "commutershed." In *Oakwood at Madison* v. *Township of Madison,* A 80/81-75 (A-52/53-74), the Court noted the region as "the area from which, in view of available employment and transportation, the population of the township would be drawn absent invalidly exclusionary zoning..." In many other exclusionary zoning cases the work/residents/trip destination form the basis of the housing region from which fair share allocations could then be made.

106

HOUSING UNIT	A room or group of rooms used by one or more individuals living separately from others in the structure, with direct access to the outside or to a public hall and containing separate toilet and kitchen facilities. *See* DWELLING UNIT.
HUMUS	Decomposed organic material.
HYDROLOGY	The science dealing with the properties, distribution and circulation of water and snow.

I

IMPACT ANALYSIS	A study to determine the effect of a proposed development on activities, utilities, circulation, surrounding land uses, community facilities, environment and other factors directly, indirectly or potentially affected.

Comment: The analysis also can include fiscal, aesthetic, social, and legal impacts. |
| **IMPEDANCE** | The rate at which a substance can absorb and transmit sound. |
| **IMPERMEABLE** | Not permitting the passage of water. |
| **IMPERVIOUS SURFACE** | Any material which reduces and prevents absorption of storm water into previously undeveloped land.

Comment: Retention and detention basins and drywells allowing water to percolate directly into the ground usually are not considered impervious surfaces. Another method by which impervious surfaces can be defined is in terms of a percolation rate in minutes/inch. For example, the New Jersey State *Standards for Construction of Individual Subsurface Sewage Disposal Systems* defines impervious formations as having a percolation rate slower than 120 minutes/inch. |
| **IMPLEMENTATION** | Carrying out or fulfilling plans and proposals. |
| **IMPOUNDMENT** | A body of water, such as a pond, confined by a dam, dike, floodgate or other barrier. |

107

 **IMPROVED LOT** A lot containing an improvement.

IMPROVEMENT Any man-made, immovable item which becomes part of, placed upon, or is affixed to, real estate.

INCENTIVE ZONING The granting by the local authority of additional development capacity in exchange for the developer's provision of a public benefit or amenity.

Comment: In New York City, developers are granted additional height and floor area in exchange for the development of public plazas and similar urban open spaces. In some developing suburbs, developers are offered additional dwelling unit density if the added units are subsidized or otherwise made available to low- and moderate-income families.

The local ordinance would have to clearly spell out the incentives. For example, a zoning ordinance allowing a density of 15 units per acre for garden apartments could include a 20% incentive (18 units/acre) if the additional units were designated for low-and moderate-income family use.

INCINERATION The controlled process by which solid, liquid or gaseous combustible wastes are burned and changed into gases and residue containing little or no combustible material.

INCINERATOR An engineered apparatus used to burn waste substances and in which all the combustion factors, temperature, retention time, turbulence and combustion air, can be controlled.

INCLUSIONARY ZONING Regulations which increase housing choice by providing the opportunity to construct more affordable, diverse and economical housing to meet the needs of low- and moderate-income families.

Comment: Inclusionary techniques include specific requirements for a minimum percentage of low- and moderate-income housing as part of any development, density bonuses for low and moderate units, and removal or modification of regulations to eliminate requirements unrelated or in excess of those needed for safe and sanitary housing. For a fuller discussion of this complex subject, see David Listokin's *Fair Share Housing Allocation* (New Brunswick, N.J.: The Center for Urban

Policy Research, 1976) and Babcock and Bosselman's *Exclusionary Zoning, Land Use Regulations and Housing in the 1970's* (New York, N.Y.: Praeger Publishing, 1973).

INDIRECT SOURCE

An indirect pollution source that by its nature attracts large numbers of polluting sources while not actually releasing the pollutant itself.

INDIVIDUAL SEWAGE DISPOSAL SYSTEM

A system for the disposal of sanitary sewage in the ground, which is so designed and constructed as to treat sewage in a manner that will retain most of the settleable solids in a septic tank and discharge the liquid portion to an adequate disposal field. *See Figure 30.*

INDOOR TENNIS FACILITY

A building or structure containing one or more roofed and enclosed tennis courts.

INDUSTRIAL PARK

A large tract of land that has been planned, developed and operated as an integrated facility for a number of individual industrial uses, with special attention to circulation, parking, utility needs, aesthetics, and compatibility.

Comment: A good reference for industrial park development standards is the *Industrial Development Handbook,* Community Builders Handbook Series, Urban Land Institute, 1979.

INDUSTRIAL PROPERTY

Any lot of land containing an industrial use or building of such uses as may be defined in the ordinance.

INDUSTRIAL SEPARATOR

An air pollution control device that uses the principle of inertia to remove particulate matter from a stream of air or gas.

INDUSTRIAL WASTE

Liquid, gaseous, chemical and solid residue or byproducts of an industrial process.

INDUSTRY

Those fields of economic activity including forestry, fishing, hunting and trapping; mining; construction; manufacturing; transportation, communication, electric, gas, and sanitary services; and wholesale trade.

INDUSTRY, LIGHT

See LIGHT INDUSTRY.

109

IN-FILL DEVELOPMENT

See ODD-LOT DEVELOPMENT.

 **INFILTRATION**

The flow of a fluid into a substance through pores or small openings.

Comment: Commonly used in hydrology to describe the flow of water into soil material. Also describes storm water inflow into a sanitary sewer system.

 **INFRASTRUCTURE**

Facilities and services needed to sustain industry, residential and commercial activities.

Comment: Infrastructure includes water and sewer lines, streets and roads, communications, and public facilities such as fire houses, parks, etc.

 **INGRESS**

Access or entry.

INN

A commercial facility for the housing and feeding of transients.

Comment: An inn is commonly distinguished from a hotel or motel by its size and its more personal atmosphere. Inns often are contained in whole or in part in buildings which were previously private residences. *See* HOTEL and MOTEL.

INSTITUTIONAL USE

A nonprofit or quasi-public use or institution such as a church, library, public, or private school, hospital, or municipally owned or operated building, structure or land used for public purpose.

 **INTERCEPTOR SEWER**

Sewers used to collect the flows from main and trunk sewers and carry them to a central point for treatment and/or discharge.

 **INTERCHANGE**

A grade separated system of access to and from major highways. *See Figure 32.*

INTERESTED PARTY

(1) In a criminal or quasi-criminal proceeding, any citizen of the state; (2) In a civil proceeding, in any court or in an administrative proceeding before a municipal agency, any individual whether residing within or without the municipality, whose right to use, acquire or enjoy property is or may be affected by any action taken under any law of the muncipality or state or the United States.

110

INTERIOR LOT

See LOT, INTERIOR.

INTERMEDIATE CARE FACILITY

A facility which provides, on a regular basis, health-related care and services to individuals who do not require the degree of care and treatment which a hospital or skilled nursing facility is designated to provide, but who, because of their mental or physical condition, require care and services (above the level of room and board) which can be made available to them only through institutional facilities such as these.

Comment: Most states regulate intermediate care facilities, which are often grouped under the general term of nursing home or long-term care facility. Intermediate care facilities are usually groups by levels; a level A facility might offer at least 2.5 hours of nursing care daily, while in a level B facility, patients would receive at least 1.25 hours daily. *See* LONG-TERM CARE FACILITY and NURSING HOME.

INTERSECTION

Where two or more roads cross at grade. *See* JUNCTION. *See Figure 32.*

INTERSTATE HIGHWAY SYSTEM

A country-wide, federally supported network of controlled and limited access highways.

INTERSTATE WATERS

(1) Rivers, lakes and other waters that flow across or form a part of state or international boundaries; (2) Waters of the Great Lakes; (3) Coastal waters including ocean waters seaward to the territorial limits and waters along the coastline (including inland streams) influenced by the tide.

INTERTIDAL AREA

The land area between high and low tide, also called a beach. *See* BEACH.

INVERSE CONDEMNATION

The taking of private property as a result of governmental activity without any formal exercise of eminent domain.

Comment: An example of an inverse condemnation is the expansion of an airport flight path which brings airplanes so low over residences so as to make them uninhabitable.

INVERSION

An atmospheric condition where a layer of cool air is trapped by a layer of warm air so that it cannot rise.

111

Comment: Inversions spread polluted air horizontally rather than vertically so that contaminating substances cannot be dispersed widely.

 ISLAND

(1) A land area totally surrounded by water; (2) In parking lot design, built-up structures, usually curbed, placed at the end of parking rows as a guide to traffic and also used for landscaping, signing or lighting.

 ISOLATED LOT

An undeveloped substandard lot in separate ownership from surrounding property.

Comment: The isolated lot invariably becomes the subject of a variance application. A New Jersey Supreme Court decision (*Chirechello* v. *Zoning Board of Adjustment,* Borough of Monmouth Beach, January 22, 1979) offers some guidelines on how to deal with the problem. The Court suggested three criteria to determine hardship:

1. Did the owner purchase the property knowing either in fact or constructively of the deficiency? For example, if the lot became nonconforming by reason of a change in the zoning regulations after the property was purchased, the owner could not know of the potential disablement.

2. Was an offer made to purchase the property at a fair price? If so, there is no hardship. (The Court indicated that the fair market value should be based on the assumption that the variance would be granted. Otherwise, the value of the unuseable lot would be zero.)

3. Conversely, can vacant land be purchased at a fair price which would make the lot conforming?

In addition to proving hardship, the applicant also must satisfy the negative criteria—adverse impact, status of property when first purchased, character of area, etc.

J

 JOINT OWNERSHIP

The equal estate interest of two or more persons.

JOURNEY TO WORK   The worker's daily trip from residence to place of employment and back, by whatever mode or modes of transportation.

JUNCTION   A place of joining or crossing of streets or railroads. *See* INTERSECTION.

JUNK   Any scrap, waste, reclaimable material or debris, whether or not stored or used in conjunction with dismantling, processing, salvage, storage, baling, disposal or other use or disposition.

Comment: Junk includes vehicles, tires, vehicle parts, equipment, paper, rags, metal, glass, building materials, household applicances, brush, wood and lumber. *See* FOOD WASTE and GARBAGE.

JUNKYARD   Any area, lot, land, parcel, building or structure or part thereof used for the storage, collection, processing, purchase, sale or abandonment of wastepaper, rags, scrap metal or other scrap or discarded goods, materials, machinery or two or more unregistered, inoperable motor vehicles or other type of junk.

JUST COMPENSATION   Payment made to a private property owner by an agency with power of eminent domain when the private property is taken for public use.

K

KENNEL   An establishment in which more than six dogs or domesticated animals more than one year old are housed, groomed, bred, boarded, trained or sold.

Comment: Since kennels include dog runs, care must be taken in locating them away from residential areas and providing noise buffers or barriers.

KIOSK   A free-standing structure upon which temporary information and/or posters, notices and announcements are posted. *See Figure 13.*

113

L

LABOR FORCE

All the population sixteen years of age or older, having the potential for active work for wages.

LAGOON

In waste water treatment, a shallow, artifical pond where sunlight, bacterial action and oxygen interact to restore waste water to a reasonable state of purity.

LAKE

An inland water body fed by springs or surrounding drainage.

LAND

Ground, soil or earth including structures on, above or below the surface.

LAND BANK

Government purchased land held for future use and development.

LAND DISTURBANCE

Any activity involving the clearing, cutting, excavating, filling, or grading of land or any other activity which alters land topography or vegetative cover.

LAND RECLAMATION

Increasing land use capability by changing the land's character or environment through drainage and/or fill. *See* FILLING.

LAND SURVEYOR

One who is licensed by the State as a land surveyor and is qualified to make accurate field measurements and mark, describe, and define land boundaries.

LAND USE

A description of how land is occupied or utilized.

LAND USE INTENSITY (LUI) STANDARDS

A system of bulk regulations, designed primarily for large scale developments, and based on the physical relationship between specific development factors.

Comment: Details of the system of land use intensity standards are outlined in the 1973 edition of HUD's *Minimum Property Standards* series, specifically in Volume 2, *Multifamily Housing,* and Volume 4, *Manual of Acceptable Practices to the HUD Minimum Property Standards.*

114

 LAND USE PLAN

A plan showing the existing and proposed location, extent and intensity of development of land to be used in the future for varying types of residential, commercial, industrial, agricultural, recreational, educational and other public and private purposes or combination of purposes.

Comment: Land use plans usually include a statement of the standards of population density and development intensity recommended for the plan area. The plan should be based on other master plan elements and natural conditions, including, but not necessarily limited to, topography, soil conditions, water supply, drainage, flood plain areas, marshes, and woodlands.

 LANDFILL

See SANITARY LANDFILL.

 LANDMARK

(1) Any site, building, structure, or natural feature that has visual, historic or cultural significance; (2) A permanent marker designating property boundaries.

 LANDSCAPE

(1) An expanse of natural scenery; (2) The addition of lawns, trees, plants, and other natural and decorative features to land.

Comment: Landscape treatment can include walks, patios and some elements of street furniture. Natural materials often are referred to as "soft" landscape, and other materials are known as "hard" landscape.

LARGE LOT ZONING

Low density residential development which requires a large parcel of land (usually more than one acre) for each dwelling.

LATERAL SEWERS

Pipes conducting sewerage from individual buildings to larger pipes called trunk or interceptor sewers that usually are located in street rights-of-way.

LAUNDROMAT

An establishment providing washing, drying or dry cleaning machines on the premises for rental use to the general public for family laundering or dry cleaning purposes.

LEACHATE

Liquid that has percolated through solid waste or other mediums from which dissolved or suspended materials have been extracted.

115

▲ LEACHING

The process by which soluble materials in the soil, such as nutrients, pesticide chemicals or contaminants, are washed into a lower layer of soil or are dissolved and carried away by water.

⬛▶▆▲ LEASE

A contractural agreement for the use of lands, structures, buildings or parts thereof for a fixed time and consideration.

⬛ LEAST COST HOUSING

Minimum standard conventional housing built in accordance with local codes and ordinances which have been carefully screened to eliminate requirements not related to health, safety, and welfare.

Comment: Some of the requirements found to be unrelated to health, safety, and welfare are large lot zoning, densities lower than 12 units per acre for multi-family, oversized utilities or infrastructures (30-foot wide streets, for example) and similar features. However, the appropriate minimum standards for lot size, density, utilities and other requirements may vary between and even within a municipality depending upon existing natural and man-made constraints, and the character of local development.

⬛▶▆▲ LESS-THAN-FEE ACQUISITION

See EASEMENTS.

⬛ LIFE CYCLE

The phases, changes or stages an organism passes through during its lifetime.

▲ LIFT

In a sanitary landfill, a compacted layer of solid waste and the top layer of cover material.

⬛ LIGHT INDUSTRY

Industrial uses which meet the performance standards, bulk controls, and other requirements established in this ordinance.

Comment: Most zoning ordinances define light industry in terms of the finished product, raw materials, or size of the machinery employed in the process. For example, *small* machine parts or *small* electronic equipment; or no motors in excess of 10 horsepower. Light industry, however, should be defined in terms of the impact of the facility on surrounding areas. A 500,000-square-foot plant turning out small machine parts would have a large

116

impact on the community. With the advent of stricter environmental laws affecting noise, air pollution, glare, etc., the difference essentially narrows down to traffic and building bulk. The above definition suggests that all industries should be required to meet the performance and bulk standards established in the ordinance and that the difference between light industry and heavy industry is essentially one of the size of the work force, size of the building, and the fact that all aspects of the industrial process are carried on within the building itself. This latter provision would rule out, for example, those facilities that require large structures outside principal buildings such as refineries, etc. In addition, by establishing a maximum size for the lot (possibly five acres), a maximum height of two stories, and a maximum floor area ratio of .5 or less, the community is assured that the industrial process generates a minimum amount of traffic and certain industries requiring tall structures are precluded.

Additional requirements could be established to further define light and heavy industry. For example, many states allow municipalities to impose higher performance standards than those established in state law. Noise standards could be established that prohibit any noise above a certain decibel rating beyond the walls of the building. Air pollution requirements could be doubled if various state laws permit municipality regulations to be more strict than the state's. However, given the difficulty in enforcing the standards and determining when violations take place, the most practical approach is to establish a maximum lot size, building height, floor area ratio, and require all facilities to be within the building. The intensity of development, by adhering to these requirements, would be restricted severely.

  LIGHT PLANE   *See* SKY EXPOSURE PLANE.

 LIMNOLOGY   The study of the physical, chemical, meteorological and biological aspects of fresh waters.

 **LINES**   *See* LOT LINES.

 LITTORAL   Pertaining to the shore of seas and oceans.

 LITTORAL DRIFT   The transportation of grains of sand due to water action produced by winds and currents.

117

LITTORAL LAND — Land that abuts a large body of water such as an ocean or sea.

LOADING SPACE — An off-street space or berth used for the loading or unloading of commercial vehicles.

LOCAL AUTHORITY — Any city, town, village or other legally authorized agency charged with administration and enforcement of land use regulations. *See* MUNICIPALITY.

LOCAL HOUSING AUTHORITY — Any public body authorized to engage in the development or administration of subsidized or public housing.

LOCAL IMPROVEMENT — A public improvement provided to a specific area which benefits that area and which is usually paid for by special assessment of benefitting property owners.

LODGE — (1) A building or group of buildings under single management, containing both rooms and dwelling units available for temporary rental to transient individuals or families; (2) The place where members of a local chapter of an association hold their meetings; and, the local chapter itself.

LODGER — A transient renter whose meals may or may not be included in the cost of his rent. *See* BOARDER.

LODGING HOUSE — A facility in which rental sleeping accommodations are provided and which meals also may be supplied as part of the fee. *See* BOARDING HOUSE.

LONG-TERM CARE FACILITY — An institution or a distinct part of an institution which is licensed or approved to provide health care under medical supervision for 24 or more consecutive hours to two or more patients who are not related to the governing authority or its members by marriage, blood or adoption.

Comment: A long-term care facility may be either a skilled nursing facility, where patients receive above a certain number of hours of nursing care daily (New Jersey requires 2.75 hours), or intermediate care facility, where patients receive less than the established number of hours of nursing care daily. In addition to a nursing home, other long-term care facilities are governmental medical institutions, or nursing units in a home for the

118

aged. *See* Extended Care Facility, Intermediate Care Facility and Nursing Home.

LOT

A designated parcel, tract or area of land established by plat, subdivision, or as otherwise permitted by law, to be used, developed or built upon as a unit. *See Figure 22.*

LOT AREA

The total area within the lot lines of a lot, excluding any street rights-of-way.

LOT AVERAGING

A design technique permitting one or more lots in a subdivision to be undersized providing the same number of lots in the same subdivision are oversized by an equal or greater area.

Comment: Lot averaging is similar to clustering except there is no common open space. It is particularly useful where topography or other environmental constraints affect the land. The ordinance should establish a maximum permitted reduction such as not more than 25% of the minimum required lot area.

LOT, CORNER

A lot or parcel of land abutting upon two or more streets at their intersection, or upon two parts of the same street forming an interior angle of less than 135 degrees. *See Figure 18.*

LOT COVERAGE

That portion of the lot that is covered by buildings and structures.

Comment: Some definitions expand this to include all other manmade improvements on the ground surface which are more impervious than the natural surface, such as paving, driveways, etc.

LOT DEPTH

The distance measured from the front lot line to the rear lot line. *See Figure 18.*

Comment: For lots where the front and rear lot lines are not parallel, the lot depth should be measured by drawing lines from the front to rear lot lines, at right angles to the front lot line, every ten feet and averaging the length of these lines.

LOT, DOUBLE FRONTAGE

See Lot, Through.

119

⬛▮	**LOT, FLAG**	*See* FLAG, LOT.
⬛▮▮	**LOT FRONTAGE**	The length of the front lot line measured at the street right-of-way line. *See Figure 20.*
⬛▮▮	**LOT, INTERIOR**	A lot other than a corner lot. *See Figure 18.*
⬛▮▮	**LOT, ISOLATED**	*See* ISOLATED LOT.
⬛▮▮	**LOT LINE**	A line of record bounding a lot which divides one lot from another lot or from a public or private street or any other public space. *See Figure 20.*
⬛▮▮	**LOT LINE, FRONT**	The lot line separating a lot from a street right-of-way. *See Figure 20.*
⬛▮▮	**LOT LINE, REAR**	The lot line opposite and most distant from the front lot line; or in the case of triangular or otherwise irregularly shaped lots, a line ten feet in length entirely within the lot, parallel to and at a maximum distance from the front lot line. *See Figure 20.*

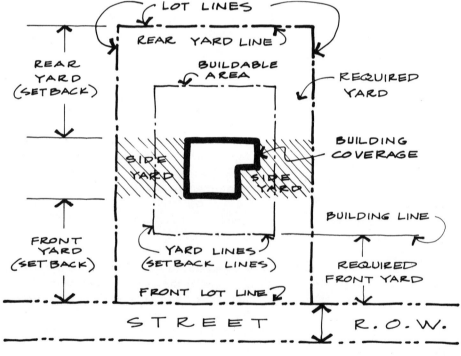

Figure 20

120

LOT LINE, SIDE	Any lot line other than a front or rear lot line. *See Figure 18.*
LOT, MINIMUM AREA OF	The smallest lot area established by the zoning ordinance on which a use or structure may be located in a particular district.
LOT OF RECORD	A lot which exists as shown or described on a plat or deed in the records of the local registry of deeds.
LOT, REVERSE FRONTAGE	A through lot which is not accessible from one of the parallel or non-intersecting streets upon which it fronts. *See Figure 34.*
LOT, THROUGH	A lot which fronts upon two parallel streets, or which fronts upon two streets which do not intersect at the boundaries of the lot. *See Figure 18.*
LOT, TRANSITION	(1) A lot in a transition zone; (2) A lot between two zoning districts permitting the same uses as allowed in each zone but with different areas and/or dimensions.

Comment: The zoning ordinance normally would establish an intermediate size for the transition lot. For example, if located between a 40,000 square foot residential zone and a 20,000 square foot residential zone, the transition lot might be required to have a minimum of 30,000 square feet. The transition lot also might be part of a lot averaging design.

LOT WIDTH	The horizontal distance between the side lines of a lot measured at right angles to its depth along a straight line parallel to the front lot line at the minimum required building setback line. *See Figure 18.*
LOW-INCOME HOUSING	Housing that is economically feasible for families whose income level is categorized as low within the standards promulgated by the United States Department of Housing and Urban Development or the appropriate state housing agency.

Comment: Generally speaking, low-income is defined as 50% or less of the median family income for a particular market area, and economically feasible is defined as housing costs between 25%–30% of gross family income.

121

M

MADE LAND

Land previously unsuitable for development because of high water table, flooding, unstable subsurface conditions or similar impairments and made suitable by corrective action. *See* FILLING and LAND RECLAMATION.

MAGNET STORE

The largest retail establishment in a shopping center which draws customers and thereby generates business for surrounding stores. *See* ANCHOR TENANT.

MAINTENANCE GUARANTEE

Any security which may be required and accepted by a governmental agency to assure that necessary improvements will function as required for a specific period of time. *See* PERFORMANCE GUARANTEE.

Comment: The maintenance guarantee takes effect after the municipality has accepted the improvements. The maintenance guarantee usually runs for a period of one to two years. If something malfunctions, the obligor is required to correct the deficiency. *See* PERFORMANCE GUARANTEE.

MALL

(1) A shaded walk or public promenade; (2) A shopping center where stores front on both sides of a pedestrian way which may be enclosed or open.

MANUFACTURING

Establishments engaged in the mechanical or chemical transformation of materials or substances into new products including the assembling of component parts, the manufacturing of products, and the blending of materials such as lubricating oils, plastics, resins or liquors.

Comment: The term manufacturing covers all mechanical or chemical transformations, whether the new product is finished or semifinished as raw material in some other process. Manufacturing production usually is carried on for the wholesale market rather than for direct sales. Processing on farms is not classified as manufacturing if the raw material is grown on the farm. The manufacturing is accessory to the major use of farming.

122

 **MAP, CONTOUR**

A map that displays land elevations in graphic form.

 MAP, OFFICIAL

See OFFICIAL MAP.

MARINA

A facility for storing, servicing, fueling, berthing and securing of pleasure boats and which may include eating, sleeping and retail facilities for owners, crews and guests.

MARKETABILITY STUDY

A study that measures the economic demand for a particular site and/or land use.

 MARQUEE

Any hood, canopy, awning or permanent construction which projects from a wall of a building, usually above an entrance.

Comment: Marquees are usually exempted from the setback requirements and allowed to project over the sidewalk, particularly in central business districts. Consideration should be given, however, to potential problems with fire-fighting and the need to get ladders and equipment above the first floor. Also, there is a matter of aesthetics and any permanent marquees extending along the sidewalk in the central business district should be undertaken in accordance with a plan to assure a continuity of colors and uniformity of construction.

 MARSHLANDS

Low-lying tracts of soft, wet lands characterized by high water tables and extensive vegetation peculiar to and characteristic of wet places.

MASKING

Covering over of one sound or element by another.

Comment: Masking is the amount the audibility threshold of one sound is raised by the presence of a second masking sound. Also used in regard to odors.

 MASS TRANSIT

A public common carrier transportation system having established routes and schedules.

MASTER DEED

A legal instrument under which title to real estate is conveyed and by which a condominium is created and established.

Comment: The master deed is the key document in establishing a condominium. It is required to be filled in the office of the county recording officer. The contents of the master deed are usually prescribed by the appropriate

123

State legislation covering condominium ownership. Such master deeds usually contain the following information: a statement placing the land described in the master deed under the provisions of the condominium act; the official title of the condominium; a legal description of the land; a survey of the land showing the improvements to be erected, common elements, and units to be sold, in sufficient detail and shown in their respective locations with dimensions; identification of each unit; a description of the common elements and limited common elements, if there are any; the proportion of undivided interests in the common elements including rights of owners; by-laws; methods of amending and supplementing the master deed; the name and nature of the association; the manner of sharing common expenses; and whatever other provisions may be desired such as restrictions or limitations of use, occupancy, transfer leasing, or other disposition of a unit, or the limitations on the use of common elements.

 **MASTER PLAN**

A comprehensive long-range plan intended to guide the growth and development of a community or region and one that includes analysis, recommendations and proposals for the community's population, economy, housing, transportation, community facilities and land use.

 **MEAN**

The average of a number of figures computed by adding up all the figures and dividing by the number of figures.

 **MEAN HIGH WATER LINE**

The line formed by the intersection of the tidal plane of mean high tide with the shore.

 **MECHANICAL TURBULENCE**

The erratic movement of air caused by local obstructions such as buildings.

 **MEDIAN**

The middle number in a series of items in which fifty percent of all figures are above the median and fifty percent are below.

 **MEDIAN ISLAND**

A barrier placed between lanes of traffic flowing in opposite directions. *See* BARRIER. *See Figure 32.*

MEDICAL BUILDING

A building that contains establishments dispensing health services. *See* HEALTH SERVICES.

MEGALOPOLIS

An extended metropolitan area created from the merging of once separate and distinct metropolitan areas.

124

MEMBERSHIP ORGANIZATION

An organization operating on a membership basis with pre-established formal membership requirements and with the intent to promote the interests of its members. Such an organization includes trade associations, professional organizations, unions, and similar political and religious organizations.

Comment: This general category excludes business establishments operated by membership organizations such as a hotel association. These are classified under the major industrial heading. *See* CLUB and FRATERNAL ORGANIZATION.

MESOTROPHIC LAKES

Lakes which are intermediate in characteristics between oligotrophic and eutrophic lakes. *See* OLIGOTROPHIC LAKES and EUTROPHIC LAKES.

METER

A metric scale measure equal to 3.28 feet.

METES AND BOUNDS

A method of describing the boundaries of land by directions and distances from a known point of reference.

METRIC SYSTEM

A decimal system of weights and measures.

METROPOLIS

The major city in a designated area; generally, any large city.

METROPOLITAN AREA

An area whose economic and social life is influenced by a metropolis and whose boundaries are roughly defined by the commuting limits to the center city.

MEZZANINE

A partial story between two full stories. *See Figure 3.*

MGD

Millions of gallons per day.

MID-RISE

See DWELLING, MID-RISE.

MIGRATION

The movement of people from one domicile to another.

Comment: The key word is domicile. It implies a permanent, as opposed to a temporary movement such as daily commuting to a job.

MILE

A linear measure equal to 5,280 feet, 1,760 yards or 1.6 kilometers.

125

▦		**MILL**	One-tenth of a cent.

Comment: The term is still used in matters relating to taxes.

MINE — (1) A cavity in the earth from which minerals and ores are extracted; (2) The act of removing minerals and ores.

MINERAL RIGHTS — One of a number of distinct and separate rights associated with real property which gives the owner of rights certain specified privileges such as to extract, sell, and receive royalties with respect to the minerals.

Comment: The holder of mineral rights, in some cases, may be able to exercise those rights to the detriment of all other rights. For example, if the mineral rights owner has the right to explore or mine the minerals, it could severely affect the remainder of the land.

MINI-MALL — A shopping center of between 80,000 to 150,000 square feet on a site of 8 to 15 acres where tenants are located on both sides of a covered walkway with direct pedestrian access to all establishments from the walkway.

Comment: Mini-malls usually function as neighborhood shopping centers or specialty shopping centers. Mini-malls usually do not require an anchor store. *See* SHOPPING CENTER and SPECIALTY SHOPPING CENTER.

MINIMUM HABITABLE FLOOR AREA — The total floor area of all the habitable rooms in a dwelling unit.

MINING — The extraction of minerals including: solids, such as coal and ores; liquids, such as crude petroleum; and gases, such as natural gases. The term also includes quarrying; well operation; milling, such as crushing, screening, washing and floatation; and other preparation customarily done at the mine site or as part of a mining activity.

MINI-WAREHOUSE — A structure containing separate storage spaces of varying sizes leased or rented on an individual basis.

Comment: Spaces are usually 30 to 400 square feet with direct access to paved driveways. The structures are usually one-story structures and resemble a series of attached garages. The space is often used to store inactive business records, household goods and even antique cars or recreation vehicles. In zones where permitted, the regulations should specify height (one story usually), distance between structures and width of driveways (15 feet), and whether outdoor storage is permitted (some allow boats and similar large items). The regulations should specify whether the space can be used for other than storage (rock and roll rehearsal halls, for example), and security measures such as lights, resident manager and fences, should be considered. *See* WAREHOUSE.

MIST

Liquid particles suspended in air and formed by condensation of vaporized liquids.

MIXED LIQUOR

A mixture of activated sludge and water containing organic matter and undergoing activated sludge treatment in an aeration tank.

MIXED USE DEVELOPMENT (MXD)

The development of a tract of land or building or structure with two or more different uses such as, but not limited to, residential, office, manufacturing, retail, public, or entertainment, in a compact urban form.

Comment: An early example of mixed use development is Rockefeller Center. But the widespread appearance of developments with several mutually supporting activities in a single, compactly configured real estate project is a very recent innovation in urban land use, dating only from the mid-1950's. Examples are Penn Center in Philadelphia (1953), Midtown Plaza in Rochester (1956) and Charles Center in Baltimore (1957). For additional information a good source is *Mixed-Use Developments: New Ways of Land Use,* Urban Land Institute, 1976.

MIXED USE ZONING

Regulations which permit a combination of different uses within a single development.

MOBILE HOME

A structure, transportable in one or more sections, which is at least 8 feet in width and 32 feet in length, which is built on a permanent chassis and designed to be used as a dwelling unit, with or without a permanent foundation when connected to the required utilities.

MOBILE HOME PARK

A site with required improvements and utilities for the long-term parking of mobile homes which may include services and facilities for the residents.

127

Comment: Mobile home parks often are licensed by the municipality or county, and compliance with regulations is a prerequisite to annual license renewal. The regulations may specify a minimum area for mobile home spaces; i.e., 4,000–5,000 square feet, and other required amenities. The spaces may be rented, owned individually, or sold as condominiums. Mobile home parks usually bar recreational vehicles, campers, or trailers.

 MOBILE HOME SPACE

A plot of land for placement of a single mobile home within a mobile home park. *See* PAD.

 MOBILE SOURCE

A moving source of pollution such as an automobile.

 MODAL SPLIT

The separation of particular modes of travel for a particular type of conveyance.

Comment: The description of a modal split of commuting traffic might indicate 85% private auto, 10% bus, and 5% pedestrian.

 MODE

In statistics, the value or number that occurs most frequently in a given series.

 MODERATE-INCOME HOUSING

Housing that is economically feasible for families whose income level is categorized as moderate within the standards promulgated by the United States Department of Housing and Urban Development or the appropriate state housing agency.

Comment: Generally speaking, moderate income is defined as between 50% and 80% of the median family income for a particular market area, and economically feasible is defined as between 25% and 30% of gross family income.

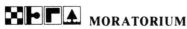 MORATORIUM

The legally authorized delay of new construction or development.

 MORBIDITY RATE

The incidence of a specific disease per specified unit of population.

 MORGUE

A place for the storage of human bodies prior to autopsy, burial or release to survivors.

 MORTALITY RATE

The annual number of deaths per thousand population.

MORTUARY	A place for the storage of human bodies prior to their burial or cremation.

MOTEL — An establishment providing transient accommodations containing six or more rooms with at least 25% of all rooms having direct access to the outside without the necessity of passing through the main lobby of the building.

MOTION PICTURE THEATER — A place where motion pictures are shown to the public for a fee.

MOTOR FREIGHT TERMINAL — A building or area in which trucks, including tractor or trailer units, are parked, stored, or serviced, including the transfer, loading or unloading of goods. A terminal may include facilities for the temporary storage of loads prior to transshipment.

MULCH — A layer of wood chips, dry leaves, straw, hay, plastic or other material placed on the surface of the soil around plants to retain moisture, prevent weeds from growing, to hold soil in place, and to aid in plant growth.

MULCHING — The application of mulch.

MULTIFAMILY DWELLING — *See* DWELLING, MULTIFAMILY.

MULTIPHASE DEVELOPMENT — A development project that is constructed in stages, each stage being capable of existing independently of the others.

MULTIUSE BUILDING — A building containing two or more distinct uses.

Comment: A multiuse building might include retail stores on the first floor and apartments on the upper floors.

MUNICIPALITY — The specific unit of government which will adopt and enforce the development ordinance.

Comment: The development regulations would, under this definition, note the specific legal name of the municipality. In some states, the county or the state itself may adopt and enforce development regulations. *See* LOCAL AUTHORITY.

129

N

NATIONAL ENVIRONMENTAL POLICY ACT

An act passed in 1974 establishing federal legislation for national environmental policy, a council on environmental quality, and the requirements for environmental impact statements.

NATIONAL FLOOD INSURANCE PROGRAM

A federal program which authorizes the sale of federally subsidized flood insurance in communities where such flood insurance is not available privately.

NATIONAL HISTORIC PRESERVATION ACT

A 1966 federal law that established a National Register of Historic Places, the Advisory Council on Historic Preservation and authorizing grants in aid for historic properties preservation.

NATIONAL REGISTER OF HISTORIC PLACES

The official list, established by the National Historic Preservation Act, of sites, districts, buildings, structures and objects significant in the nation's history or whose artistic or architectural value is unique.

NATIONAL WILD AND SCENIC RIVERS SYSTEM

Rivers designated by a state or Congress as having outstanding national scenic or historic value.

Comment: Rivers so designated must be administered in a manner which protects and enhances their scenic or historic significance.

NATURAL DRAINAGE FLOW

The pattern of surface and storm water drainage from a particular site before the construction or installation of improvements or prior to any regrading.

NATURAL GRADE

See GRADE, NATURAL.

NATURAL GROUND SURFACE

The ground surface in its original state before any grading, excavation or filling. *See* GRADE, NATURAL.

NATURAL MONUMENT

(1) A natural feature or object used to define or mark a boundary; (2) Any large, remarkable natural feature.

NATURAL RECHARGE

Adding water to the aquifer by natural means such as precipitation or from lakes and rivers.

 **NATURAL RESOURCES INVENTORY (NRI)**

A survey of the existing natural elements relating to land, water, air, plant and animal life of an area or a community and the interrelationship of these elements. The natural resources inventory usually includes soil surveys, geology, topography (including watershed and flood areas), vegetation, land use, zoning and property ownership.

Comment: The natural resources inventory is an important input to local master plan preparation, and most useful in the review of subdivision and other development plans. Although such studies can provide direction in the specific use of land, they are primarily an indication as to which areas in the community are environmentally suitable for development and which are not. Depending on study detail, they also can provide:
1. Acceptable levels of development intensity
2. Background information for the preparation of environmental impact statements
3. Disclosure of current imbalances between development and the environment
4. Information to residents on the environmental impacts of development

The NRI is a community-wide inventory and as such, its data may not be sufficiently precise for use in the detailed review of specific development projects. However, one of the initial steps in the design review procedure is a check of the proposed plans against the findings of the natural resources inventory. This check may provide some design direction, or at least alert the reviewing authority of potential environmental problems. This review also may suggest that an environmental impact statement may be necessary.

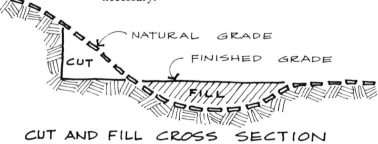

CUT AND FILL CROSS SECTION

Figure 21

 **NATURAL SELECTION**

The natural process by which organisms best adapted to their environment survive and those less well adapted are eliminated.

131

 **NEGATIVE EASEMENT**

See EASEMENT, NEGATIVE.

 NEIGHBORHOOD

An area of a community with characteristics that distinguish it from other community areas and which may include distinct ethnic or economic characteristics, schools or social clubs, or boundaries defined by physical barriers such as major highways and railroads or natural features such as rivers.

 NEIGHBORING DWELLING

Any first or second lot in either direction along the same side of the street from the subject lot, or any lot fronts directly across from the subject lot or first or second lot adjacent thereto.

Comment: The phrase is used in zoning to establish a prevailing setback line.

NET AREA OF LOT (NET ACREAGE)

The area of the lot excluding those features or areas which the development ordinance excludes from the calculations.

Comment: A development ordinance might exclude, for density or area calculation purposes, such undevelopable or critical areas of land such as floodways, areas with steep slopes, easements or similar "problem" land.

NEW CAR AGENCY

See AUTOMOBILE SALES.

NEW TOWN OR NEW COMMUNITY

A planned community, usually developed on largely vacant land and containing housing, employment, commerce, industry, recreation and open space equivalent to that of an established city or town.

Comment: The term *planned community* implies a predetermined population level and phased development over a relatively short period. Examples of new towns include Reston, Virginia and Columbia, Maryland.

  NOISE

Any undesired audible sound.

  NOISE POLLUTION

Continuous or episodic excessive noise in the human environment.

Comment: Noise pollution usually is defined in terms of a maximum decibel level by frequency range.

132

NONCONFORMING LOT

A lot, the area, dimensions or location of which was lawful prior to the adoption, revision or amendment of the zoning ordinance, but which fails by reason of such adoption, revision or amendment to conform to the present requirements of the zoning district.

NONCONFORMING SIGN

Any sign lawfully existing on the effective date of an ordinance, or an amendment thereto, which renders such sign nonconforming because it does not conform to all the standards and regulations of the adopted or amended ordinance.

NONCONFORMING STRUCTURE OR BUILDING

A structure or building the size, dimensions or location of which was lawful prior to the adoption, revision or amendment to a zoning ordinance, but which fails by reason of such adoption, revision or amendment, to conform to the present requirements of the zoning district.

NONCONFORMING USE

A use or activity which was lawful prior to the adoption, revision or amendment of a zoning ordinance, but which fails, by reason of such adoption, revision or amendment, to conform to the present requirements of the zoning district.

NON-POINT RUNOFF

Surface water entering a channel from no definable discharge source.

NUISANCE

An interference with the enjoyment and use of property.

NUISANCE ELEMENT

Any environmental pollutant, such as smoke, odors, liquid wastes, solid wastes, radiation, noise, vibration, glare or heat.

NURSERY

Land or greenhouses used to raise flowers, shrubs and plants for sale. *See* GREENHOUSE.

NURSERY SCHOOL

See CHILD CARE CENTER.

NURSING HOME

An extended or intermediate care facility licensed or approved to provide full-time convalescent or chronic care to individuals who, by reason of advanced age, chronic illness or infirmity, are unable to care for themselves.

Comment: Nursing homes are now usually referred to as long-term care facilities. *See* EXTENDED CARE FACILITY; INTERMEDIATE CARE FACILITY and LONG-TERM CARE FACILITY.

O

OBSTRUCTION

Any dam, wall, embankment, levee, dike, pile, abutment, soil material, bridge, conduit, culvert, building, wire, fence, refuse, fill, structure or other matter in, along, across or projecting into any channel, watercourse, or flood plain which may impede, retard, or change the direction of the flow of water, either in itself or by catching debris carried by such water, or that is placed where the flow of water might carry the same downstream.

OCCUPANCY OR OCCUPIED

The residing of an individual or individuals overnight in a dwelling unit, or the installation, storage or use of equipment, merchandise or machinery in any public, commercial or industrial building.

OCCUPANCY PERMIT

A required permit allowing occupancy of a building or structure after it has been determined that the building meets all the requirements of applicable ordinances.

Comment: The occupancy permit may be a temporary one for a given period of time to permit completion of certain improvements. For example, installation of landscaping may be delayed because of weather. Obviously, a temporary permit would not be granted if the unfinished or incomplete improvement is essential to the use or affects health or safety.

OCCUPANCY RATE

The ratio of occupied dwelling units to total dwelling units.

OCCUPANT

The individual or individuals in actual possession of a premises.

OCCUPATION

Gainful employment in which an individual engages to earn compensation for the necessities of life.

ODD-LOT DEVELOPMENT

The development of new housing or other buildings on scattered vacant sites in a built up area.

ODOROUS MATTER

Any material that produces an olfactory response in a human being.

Comment: This is a difficult nuisance element to monitor and enforce.

134

OFFER	A proposal to enter into an agreement with another party.
OFFICE	A room or group of rooms used for conducting the affairs of a business, profession, service, industry, or government.
OFFICE BUILDING	A building used primarily for conducting the affairs of a business, profession, service, industry or government, or like activity, that may include ancillary services for office workers such as a restaurant, coffee shop, newspaper or candy stand.

Comment: Standards for office buildings vary enormously. Typical controls include floor area ratio, height, ground coverage, and parking.

OFFICE PARK A development on a tract of land that contains a number of separate office buildings, supporting uses and open space designed, planned, constructed and managed on an integrated and coordinated basis.

OFFICE-AT-HOME A home occupation in which a part of a dwelling unit is used primarily as the resident's office. *See* HOME OCCUPATION and HOME PROFESSIONAL OFFICE.

OFFICIAL MAP A legally adopted map that conclusively shows the location and width of proposed streets, public facilities and public areas, and drainage rights-of-way.

Comment: State regulations vary as to what may be shown on an official map.

OFFICIAL SOIL MAP Maps delineating soil types and that are part of a Soil Conservation Service soil survey.

OFFICIAL SOILS INTERPRETATION The written description of soil types and their characteristics and accompanying maps which are part of a recognized soil survey.

OFF-SITE Located outside the lot lines of the lot in question but within the property (of which the lot is a part) that is the subject of a development application, or within a contiguous portion of a street or other right-of-way. *See Figure 27.*

OFF-STREET PARKING SPACE

A temporary storage area for a motor vehicle that is directly accessible to an access aisle, and which is not located on a dedicated street right-of-way. *See Figure 2.*

 **OFF-TRACT**

Not located on the property that is the subject of a development application nor on a contiguous portion of a street or other right-of-way. *See Figure 27.*

 **OLIGOTROPHIC LAKES**

Deep lakes that have a low supply of nutrients, contain little organic matter, and are characterized by high water transparency and high dissolved oxygen.

 **ONE HUNDRED PERCENT LOCATION**

A prime business location and the location usually able to command the highest commercial and office rentals for a particular area or municipality.

 **ON SITE**

Located on the lot that is the subject of an application for development. *See Figure 27.*

 **ON-STREET PARKING SPACE**

A temporary storage area for a motor vehicle which is located on a dedicated street right-of-way. *See Figure 2.*

 ON TRACT

Located on the property that is the subject of a development application or on a contiguous portion of a street or other right-of-way.

OPACITY

Degree of obscuration of light.

Comment: The range is from zero to 100%. For example, a window has zero opacity and a wall is 100% opacity. The Ringelmann system of evaluating smoke density is based on opacity.

OPEN BURNING

Uncontrolled burning of wastes in an open area.

OPEN DUMP

See DUMP.

OPEN MEETING OR HEARING

A meeting open to the public.

Comment: Open meetings may be required by statute under a "sunshine law." However, the fact that a meeting is required to be open to the public does not necessarily mean that public can participate. Public participation usually is permitted only at a public *hearing,* duly noticed and advertised.

 OPEN SPACE

Any parcel or area of land or water essentially unimproved and set aside, dedicated, designated or reserved for public or private use or enjoyment, or for the use and enjoyment of owners and occupants of land adjoining or neighboring such open space.

OPEN SPACE, COMMON

Land within or related to a development, not individually owned or dedicated for public use, which is designed and intended for the common use or enjoyment of the residents of the development and may include such complementary structures and improvements as are necessary and appropriate. *See Figure 36.*

OPEN SPACE, GREEN

An open space area not occupied by any structures or impervious surfaces.

OPEN SPACE, PRIVATE

Common open space held in private ownership, the use of which is normally limited to the occupants of a single dwelling or building.

OPEN SPACE, PUBLIC

Open space owned by a public agency and maintained by it for the use and enjoyment of the general public.

OPEN SPACE RATIO

Total area of open space divided by the total site area in which the open space is located.

OPTION

An exclusive right to purchase, rent or sell a property usually at a stipulated price and within a specified time.

ORDINANCE

A municipally adopted law or regulation.

ORGANIC

Referring to or derived from living organisms.

ORGANISM

Any living human, plant or animal.

ORIGIN AND DESTINATION STUDY

A transportation study that records the location from where a trip begins and where it will end.

OUTBUILDING

A separate accessory building or structure not physically connected to the principal building.

Comment: Outbuildings usually are smaller than the principal structure and may be used for storage or ancillary use.

137

OUTDOOR STORAGE The keeping, in an unroofed area of any goods, junk, material, merchandise, or vehicles in the same place for more than twenty-four hours.

Comment: Many ordinances prohibit outdoor storage in any required yard areas unless the outdoor storage is screened from public view by a fence or wall.

OUTFALL The mouth of a sewer, drain or conduit where an effluent is discharged into the receiving waters.

OVERFIRE AIR Air forced into the top of an incinerator to fan the flame.

OVERFLOW RIGHTS An easement that allows an owner to run excess water onto another's land.

OVERFLOWED LAND A flood plain or land subject to frequent flooding. *See* FLOOD PLAIN.

OVERHANG (1) The part of a roof or wall which extends beyond the facade of a lower wall; (2) The portion of a vehicle extending beyond the wheel stops or curb. *See Figure 13.*

Comment: In parking lot design, the depth of the parking stall can be reduced by two feet if curbing is used for wheel stops and allowance is made for the overhang. However, the overhanging car can interfere with pedestrian travel if it encroaches on an adjacent sidewalk. If the sidewalk is placed two or more feet from the curb, the intervening space is generally not appropriate for planting due to the difficulty in caring for the plants and because of oil leakage from car engines.

OWNER An individual, firm, association, syndicate, partnership, or corporation having sufficient proprietary interest to seek development of land.

OXIDATION POND A man-made lake or pond in which organic wastes are reduced by bacterial action.

OZONE A pungent, colorless, toxic gas.

Comment: Ozone is one component of photochemical smog and is considered a major air pollutant.

138

P

PACKAGE PLANT

Small, self-contained sewage treatment facilities built to serve developed areas beyond the service area of sanitary sewers.

PACKED TOWER

An air pollution control device in which polluted air is forced upward through a tower packed with crushed rock or wood chips while a liquid is sprayed downward on the packing material to dissolve the pollutants in the air stream or have the pollutants chemically react with the liquid.

PAD

A paved space in a mobile home park for the parking of a mobile home and usually containing utility connections. *See* Mobile Home Space.

PARAPET

The extension of the main walls of a building above the roof level. *See Figure 13.*

Comment: Parapet walls often are used to shield mechanical equipment and vents.

PARCEL

A lot or tract of land. *See Figure 22.*

PARK

A tract of land, designated and used by the public for active and passive recreation.

PARKING ACCESS

The area of a parking lot that allows motor vehicles ingress and egress from the street. *See Figure 2.*

PARKING AREA

Any public or private land area designed and used for parking motor vehicles including parking lots, garages, private driveways and legally designated areas of public streets. *See* Garage.

PARKING AREA, PRIVATE

A parking area for the private use of the owners or occupants of the lot on which the parking area is located.

PARKING AREA, PUBLIC

A parking area available to the public, with or without compensation, or used to accommodate clients, customers, or employees.

PARKING BAY — The parking module consisting of one or two rows of parking spaces and the aisle from which motor vehicles enter and leave the spaces. *See Figure 2.*

PARKING LOT — An off-street, ground level area, usually surfaced and improved, for the temporary storage of motor vehicles. *See* GARAGE; PARKING AREA.

PARKING SPACE — A space for the parking of a motor vehicle within a public or private parking area. *See* OFF-STREET PARKING SPACE; ON-STREET PARKING SPACE; STALL.

PAROCHIAL SCHOOL — *See* SCHOOL, PAROCHIAL.

PARTIAL TAKING — The condemnation of part of a property.

PARTICULATE LOADING — The introduction of particulates into the ambient air.

PARTICULATES — Finely divided solid or liquid particles in the air or in an emission including dust, smoke, fumes, mist, spray and fog.

PARTY DRIVEWAY — A single way providing vehicular access to two adjoining properties. *See* COMMON PASSAGEWAY. *See Figure 22.*

PARTY IMMEDIATELY CONCERNED — For purposes of notice, party immediately concerned means any applicant for development, the owners of the subject property, and all owners of property and government agencies entitled to notice under a zoning ordinance, subdivision regulations or other development controls.

PARTY WALL — A common shared wall between two separate structures, buildings, or dwelling units. *See Figure 22.*

PATH — A cleared way for pedestrians and/or bicycles which may or may not be paved.

PATHOGENIC — Causing or capable of causing disease.

PATIO — *See* TERRACE.

PAVEMENT — (1) Brick, stone, concrete or asphalt placed on the surface of the land; (2) That part of a street having an improved surface.

140

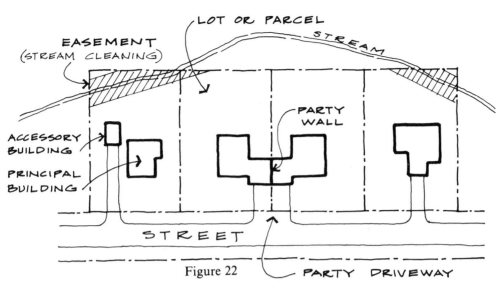

Figure 22

 **PEAK HOUR TRAFFIC**

The largest number of vehicles passing over a designated section of a street during the busiest one hour period during a 24-hour period.

 PEAT

Partially decomposed organic material.

 **PEDESTRIAN**

An individual who travels on foot.

 **PEDESTRIAN SCALE**

The proportional relationship between an individual and his or her environment.

Comment: The pedestrian scale is an informal and subjective standard. It suggests that the relationship between the person and his or her environment, whether natural or man-made, is comfortable, intimate, and contributes to the individual's sense of accessibility.

 **PEDESTRIAN TRAFFIC COUNT**

The number of people who walk past a single point during a specified period of time.

PENINSULA

A projection of land surrounded on three sides by water.

PENTHOUSE

A roofed structure located on the roof of a building. *See Figure 13.*

Comment: Penthouses may be used to house a variety of purposes; offices, dwelling units or mechanical equipment associated with a building.

PEOPLE MOVER

A conveyor system designed for carrying pedestrians.

141

PERCOLATING AREA   That portion of soil utilized as the effective disposal media for sewage.

PERCOLATION   Downward flow or infiltration of water through the pores or spaces of rock or soil.

PERCOLATION TEST   A test designed to determine the ability of ground to absorb water and used in determining the suitability of a soil for drainage or for the use of a septic system.

PERFORMANCE GUARANTEE   Any security that may be accepted by a municipality as a guarantee that improvements required as part of an application for development are satisfactorily completed.

Comment: Performance guarantees usually are partly in cash and the remainder secured with a surety bond. *See* MAINTENANCE GUARANTEE.

PERFORMANCE STANDARDS   A set of criteria or limits relating to nuisance elements which a particular use or process may not exceed.

Comment: The standards may be established by state or federal law or by the municipality. They may vary by zone or use.

PERIMETER   The boundaries or borders of a lot, tract, or parcel of land.

PERIMETER LANDSCAPED OPEN SPACE   A landscaped area intended to enhance the appearance of parking lots and other outdoor auto related uses or to screen incompatible uses from each other along their boundaries.

PERMAFROST   A permanently frozen soil layer.

PERMEABILITY   The ease with which air, water or other fluids can move through soil or rock.

PERMIT   Written governmental permission issued by an authorized official, empowering the holder thereof to do some act not forbidden by law, but not allowed without such authorization.

PERMITTED USE   Any use allowed in a zoning district and subject to the restrictions applicable to that zoning district.

PERMITTEE   Any person to whom a permit is issued.

 **PERSON**

A corporation, company, association, society, firm, partnership or joint stock company, as well as an individual, a state, and all political subdivisions of a state or any agency or instrumentality thereof.

PERSONAL SERVICES

Establishments primarily engaged in providing services involving the care of a person or his or her apparel.

Comment: Personal services usually includes the following: laundry, cleaning and garment services, garment pressing, linen supply, diaper service, coin-operated laundries, dry cleaning plants, carpet and upholstery cleaning, photographic studios, beauty shops, barber shops, shoe repair, hat cleaning, funeral services, steam baths, reducing salons and health clubs, clothing rental, locker rental porter service, etc.

 **PERVIOUS SURFACE**

Any material that permits full or partial absorption of storm water into previously unimproved land. *See* IMPERVIOUS SURFACE.

PESTICIDE

An agent used to control pests.

Comment: Pesticides include insecticides for use against harmful insects; herbicides for weed control; fungicides for control of plant disease; rodenticides for killing rats, mice, etc.; and germicides used in disinfectant products, algaecides, slimicides, etc. Some pesticides, particularly if they are misused, can contaminate water, air or soil and accumulate in man, animals and the environment.

PESTICIDE TOLERANCE

A scientifically and legally established limit for the amount of chemical residue that can be permitted to remain in or on a harvested food or feed crop as a result of the application of a chemical for pest-control purposes.

pH

A measure of the acidity or alkalinity of a material, liquid or solid.

Comment: A pH of 7 is considered neutral. Below 7 is acidic; above 7 is basic.

PHARMACY

A place where drugs and medicines are prepared and dispensed. *See* DRUG STORE.

PHENOLS

A group of organic compounds that, even in very low concentrations, produce a taste and odor in water.

143

■ **PHOTOCHEMICAL SMOG**

Air pollution associated with oxidants rather than with sulfur oxides, particulates or similar materials.

■ **PIERHEAD LINE**

A line beyond which no structure may extend into tidal waters.

■ **PIG**

A container usually made of lead and used to ship or store radioactive materials.

■ **PILE**

A nuclear reactor.

■ **PILOT PLANT**

An establishment or part thereof used to test out concepts and ideas, and determine physical layouts, material flows, types of equipment required, costs, and secure other information prior to full-scale production.

Comment: The pilot plant is usually an intermediate step between the research laboratory and full-scale production. It requires monitoring and supervision by other than the usual production personnel and may involve frequent changes in physical layout, material flows, or even processes. Pilot plants may produce production grade goods, particularly during the latter stages of the pilot plant process. However, if the pilot plant is switched to full production and operation and used for other than testing, it should be treated as a principal permitted use. Otherwise, most development ordinances allow some percentage of research facilities, usually not more than 25% of the floor area, to be used for pilot plant operations.

■ **PLANKTON**

The floating or weakly swimming plant and animal life in a body of water, often microscopic in size.

■ ■ **PLANNED COMMERCIAL DEVELOPMENT**

An area of a minimum contiguous size, as specified by ordinance, to be planned, developed, operated and maintained as a single entity containing one or more structures to accommodate commercial or office uses, or both, and appurtenant common areas and other uses incidental to the predominant uses.

■ ■ **PLANNED DEVELOPMENT**

An area of a minimum contiguous size, as specified by ordinance, developed according to plan as a single entity and containing one or more structures with appurtenant common areas.

144

| | | PLANNED INDUSTRIAL DEVELOPMENT | A planned development that accommodates industrial uses. |

PLANNED INDUSTRIAL DEVELOPMENT

A planned development that accommodates industrial uses.

PLANNED UNIT DEVELOPMENT (PUD)

An area of a minimum contiguous size, as specified by ordinance, to be planned and developed as a single entity containing one or more residential clusters or planned unit residential developments and one or more public, quasi-public, commercial or industrial areas in such ranges of ratios of nonresidential uses to residential uses as shall be specified.

PLANNED UNIT RESIDENTIAL DEVELOPMENT (PURD)

An area of a minimum contiguous size, as specified by ordinance, to be planned and developed as a single entity and containing one or more residential clusters; appropriate commercial, public or quasi-public uses may be included if such uses are primarily for the benefit of the residential development.

PLANNING BOARD

The duly designated planning board of the municipality, county, or region.

Comment: The planning board (planning commission) is created by ordinance with responsibility for reviewing and approving applications for development and preparation of master plans.

PLAT

(1) A map representing a tract of land, showing the boundaries and location of individual properties and streets; (2) A map of a subdivision or site plan.

PLAT, FINAL

The final map of all or a portion of a subdivision or site plan which is presented to the proper review authority for final approval.

Comment: Final approval usually is granted only upon the completion or installation of all improvements or the posting of performance guarantees assuring the completion or installation of such improvements.

PLAT, PRELIMINARY

A preliminary map indicating the proposed layout of the subdivision or site plan which is submitted to the proper review authority for consideration and preliminary approval.

PLAT, SKETCH

A rough sketch map of a proposed subdivision or site plan of sufficient accuracy to be used for the purpose of discussion and classification.

145

PLAZA	An open space which may be improved and landscaped; usually surrounded by streets and buildings. *See* COURT; SQUARE. *See Figure 13.*
PLOT	(1) A single unit parcel of land; (2) A parcel of land that can be identified and referenced to a recorded plat or map.
PLUME	The visible emission from a flue or chimney.
POINT SOURCE	A stationary source of a large individual emission, generally of an industrial nature. *See* AREA SOURCE; STATIONARY SOURCE.
POLLUTANT	Any introduced gas, liquid or solid that makes a resource unfit for a specific purpose.
POLLUTION	The presence of matter or energy whose nature, location or quantity produces undesired environmental effects.
PORCH	A roofed open area, which may be glazed or screened, usually attached to or part of and with direct access to or from, a building. *See Figure 26.*

Comment: A porch becomes a room when the space enclosed is heated or air conditioned and, if glazed, when the percentage of window area to wall area is less than 50%.

POROSITY	A measure of the amount of space between the grains or the cracks that can fill with water.
POTABLE WATER	Water suitable for drinking or cooking purposes.
PPM	Parts per million.

Comment: This is a unit commonly used to represent the degree of pollutant concentration where the concentrations are small. Larger concentrations often are given in percentages.

PRECIPITATE	A solid that separates from a solution because of some chemical or physical change or the formation of such a solid.
PRECIPITATION	In pollution control work, any of a number of air pollution control devices, usually using mechanical/electrical means, to collect particulates from an emission.

146

 **PRE-EMPTIVE RIGHT**

The right of a riparian owner to a preference in the acquisition of lands under tidewaters adjoining his upland.

 **PRELIMINARY APPROVAL**

Preliminary approval means the conferral of certain rights, prior to final approval, after specific elements of a development or site plan have been approved by the proper reviewing authority and agreed to by the applicant.

Comment: Most state enabling acts prescribe the rights secured by preliminary approval. It often means that the zoning and general terms and conditions of approval will not be changed for a prescribed period of time, often 3-5 years.

 PRELIMINARY FLOOR PLANS AND ELEVATIONS

Architectural drawings prepared during early and introductory stages of the design of a project, illustrating in schematic form the scope, scale and relation of the project to its site and immediate environs.

 PRELIMINARY PLAN

See PLAT, PRELIMINARY.

 PREMISES

A lot, parcel, tract or plot of land together with the buildings and structures thereon.

 PRESCRIPTION

The acquisition of land by right of continuous use without protest from the owner.

Comment: The time period for a prescription is usually twenty years. *See* CONDEMNATION; DEDICATION; RESERVATION.

 PRESERVATION, HISTORIC

See HISTORIC PRESERVATION.

 PRETREATMENT

In waste water treatment, any process used to reduce the pollution load before the waste water is introduced into a main sewer system or delivered to a treatment plant.

PRIMARY TREATMENT

The first stage in waste water treatment in which substantially all floating or settleable solids are removed by screening and sedimentation.

PRINCIPAL BUILDING

See BUILDING PRINCIPAL.

147

▣	**PRINCIPAL USE**	The primary or predominant use of any lot.
▣	**PRIVATE CLUB OR LODGE**	A building and related facilities owned or operated by a corporation, association, or group of individuals established for the fraternal, social, educational, recreational or cultural enrichment of its members and not primarily for profit, and whose members meet certain prescribed qualifications for membership and pay dues.
▣	**PRIVATE SCHOOL**	*See* SCHOOL, PRIVATE.
▲	**PROBABILITY**	A statistical method that calculates the chance a prescribed event will occur.
▲	**PROCESS WEIGHT**	The total weight of all materials, including fuels, introduced into a manufacturing process.

Comment: The process weight is used to calculate the allowable rate of emission of pollutant matter from the process.

▣	**PROCESSING**	A series of operations, usually in a continuous and regular action or succession of actions, taking place or carried on in a definite manner.

Comment: The term processing usually is associated with the chemical transformation of materials or substances into new products and may include the blending and combining of gases and liquids. However, the term also may be applied to a specific industrial or manufacturing operation such as the "open-hearth process" for manufacturing steel.

▣	**PROCESSING AND WAREHOUSING**	The storage of materials in a warehouse or terminal and where such materials may be combined, broken down or aggregated for transshipment or storage purposes where the original material is not chemically or physically changed.

Comment: Processing and warehousing is a single term and must be defined as such. Otherwise, one gets into a situation whereby the word "processing," which is akin to manufacturing, connotes a manufacturing facility which would also contain warehousing space. Obviously, it is not uncommon for a manufacturing facility to have a warehouse and shipping facilities. The term processing and warehousing as defined is essentially a storage and shipment place as opposed to a manufacturing establishment.

PROFESSIONAL OFFICE

The office of a member of a recognized profession maintained for the conduct of that profession. *See* HOME PROFESSIONAL OFFICE.

PROHIBITED USE

A use that is not permitted in a zone district.

Comment: Most ordinances are permissive ordinances and a use not specifically permitted is prohibited.

PROJECT

A development with the necessary site improvements, on a particular parcel of land.

PROJECTION

(1) A prediction of a future state based on an analysis of what has happened in the past; (2) Part of a building or structure which is exempt from the bulk requirements of the zoning ordinance.

Comment: Usually bay windows and steps may project into required yards, and mechanical equipment on roofs may exceed the height limitation.

PROPERTY LINE

See LOT LINE.

PROTECTIVE COVENANT

See RESTRICTIVE COVENANT.

PUBLIC ADMINISTRATION

Legislative, judicial, administrative and regulatory activities of federal, state, local and international governmental agencies.

Comment: Government-owned and operated business establishments are excluded from this category and are classified in accordance with the major activity.

PUBLIC AREAS

Public parks, playgrounds, trails, paths and other recreational areas and other public open spaces; scenic and historic sites; schools and other public buildings and structures.

PUBLIC DEVELOPMENT PROPOSAL

A master plan, capital improvement program or other proposal for land development, and any amendment thereto, adopted by the appropriate public body.

149

 **PUBLIC DOMAIN** All lands owned by government.

 **PUBLIC DRAINAGE WAY** The land reserved or dedicated for the installation of storm water sewers or drainage ditches, or required along a natural stream or watercourse for preserving the channel and providing for the flow of water so as to safeguard the public against flood damage, sedimentation and erosion.

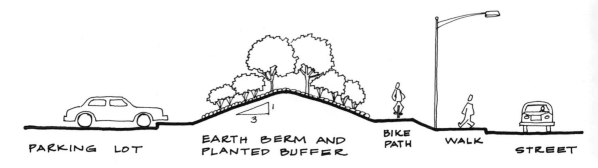

PARKING LOT   EARTH BERM AND PLANTED BUFFER   BIKE PATH   WALK   STREET

Figure 23

 **PUBLIC GARAGE** *See* GARAGE, PUBLIC.

 **PUBLIC HEARING** A meeting announced and advertised in advance and open to the public, with the public given an opportunity to talk and participate.

Comment: Public hearings often are required before adoption or implementation of a master plan, project, ordinance or like activity which will have widespread effect on the public.

 **PUBLIC HOUSING** Housing that is constructed, bought, owned, or rented and operated by a local housing authority for low-income families. *See* LOW-INCOME HOUSING; LOCAL HOUSING AUTHORITY.

 **PUBLIC IMPROVEMENT** Any improvement, facility or service together with its associated public site or right-of-way necessary to provide transportation, drainage, public or private utilities, energy or similar essential services.

 **PUBLIC NOTICE** The advertisement of a public hearing in a paper of general circulation in the area, and through other media sources, indicating the time, place and nature of the public hearing.

150

 **PUBLIC SEWER AND WATER SYSTEM**

Any system, other than an individual septic tank, tile field, or individual well, that is operated by a municipality, governmental agency, or a public utility for the collection, treatment and disposal of wastes and the furnishing of potable water.

 **PUBLIC TRANSIT SYSTEM**

Any vehicle or transportation system, owned or regulated by a governmental agency, used for the mass transport of people.

 **PUBLIC UTILITY**

A closely regulated private enterprise with an exclusive franchise for providing a public service.

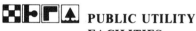 **PUBLIC UTILITY FACILITIES**

Telephone, electric and cable television lines, poles, equipment and structures; water or gas pipes, mains, valves or structures; sewer pipes, valves or structures; pumping stations; telephone exchanges and repeater stations; and all other facilities, equipment and structures necessary for conducting a service by a government or a public utility.

 PULVERIZATION

The crushing or grinding of material into small pieces.

 PUMPING STATION

A building or structure containing the necessary equipment to pump sewage to a higher level.

 PUTRESCIBLE

Capable of being decomposed by microorganisms with sufficient rapidity to cause nuisances from odors or gases.

Q

  QUADRUPLEX

See DWELLING, QUADRUPLEX.

 QUARRY

A place where rock, ore, stone and similar materials are excavated for sale or for off-tract use. *See* GRAVEL PIT; SAND PIT.

 QUARTER SECTION

A tract of land one-half-mile square, 2,640 feet by 2,640 feet, or 160 acres.

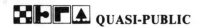 **QUASI-PUBLIC**

A use owned or operated by a nonprofit, religious or eleemosynary institution and providing educational, cultural, recreational, religious or similar types of public programs.

Comment: The term is somewhat antiquated. A quasi-public use should be included under the definition of institutional or public uses.

QUENCH TANK

A water-filled tank used to cool incinerator residues.

QUORUM

A majority of the full authorized membership of a board or agency.

R

RAD

A unit of measurement of radiation absorbed by a human.

RADIAL STREET SYSTEM

A pattern of streets in which the streets converge on a central point or area. *See Figure 35.*

RADIATION

The emission of fast atomic particles or rays by the nucleus of an atom.

Comment: Some elements are naturally radioactive while others become radioactive after bombardment with neutrons or other particles. The three major forms of radiation are alpha, beta and gamma.

RADIATION STANDARDS

Regulations that include exposure standards, permissible concentrations and regulations for transportation of radioactive material.

RAINFALL, EXCESS

The portion of rainfall which becomes direct surface runoff.

RAMP

(1) A sloping roadway or passage used to join two different levels of streets, structures or buildings; (2) Driveways leading to parking aisles.

152

RANCH	A place where livestock is bred or raised.
RASP	A device used to grate solid waste into a more manageable material, ridding it of much of its odor.
RATABLE PROPERTY	Real property subject to tax by a municipality or other taxing district.
RAVINE	A long, deep hollow in the earth's surface; a valley with sharply sloping walls created by the action of stream waters.
RAW SEWAGE	Untreated domestic or commercial waste water.
REAR YARD	*See* YARD, REAR.
REASONABLE USE DOCTRINE	A common law principle that no one has the right to use his property in a way which deprives others of the lawful enjoyment of their property.
RECEIVING WATERS	Rivers, lakes, oceans or other bodies that receive treated or untreated waste waters.
RECHARGE	The addition to, or replenishing of, water in an aquifer.
RECLAIMED LAND	*See* MADE LAND.
RECREATION, ACTIVE	Leisure time activities, usually of a more formal nature and performed with others, often requiring equipment and taking place at prescribed places, sites or fields.

Comment: The term active recreation is more a word of art than a precise definition. It obviously includes swimming, tennis and other court games, baseball and other field sports, and playground activities. There may be a legitimate difference of opinion as to whether park use per se may be considered active recreation, although obviously certain activities in parks clearly would qualify. Bike riding, hiking, walking and picnicking are usually not considered active recreation.

RECREATION FACILITY	A place designed and equipped for the conduct of sports, leisure time activities and other customary and usual recreational activities.

153

RECREATION FACILITY, COMMERCIAL	A recreation facility operated as a business and open to the public for a fee.
RECREATION FACILITY, PERSONAL	A recreation facility provided as an accessory use on the same lot as the principal permitted use and designed to be used primarily by the occupants of the principal use and their guests.
RECREATION FACILITY, PRIVATE	A recreation facility operated by a non-profit organization, and open only to bona fide members and guests of such nonprofit organization.
RECREATION FACILITY, PUBLIC	A recreation facility operated by a governmental agency and open to the general public.
RECREATION, PASSIVE	Any leisure time activity not considered active.
RECREATIONAL DEVELOPMENT	A residential development planned, maintained, operated and integrated with a major recreation facility.
RECREATIONAL VEHICLE	A vehicular type portable structure without permanent foundation, which can be towed, hauled or driven and primarily designed as temporary living accommodation for recreational, camping and travel use and including but not limited to travel trailers, truck campers, camping trailers and self-propelled motor homes.
RECREATIONAL VEHICLE PARK	*See* CAMPGROUND.
RECTILINEAR STREET SYSTEM	A pattern of streets that is characterized by right angle roadways, grid pattern blocks and four-way intersections. *See Figure 33.*
RECYCLING	The process by which waste products are reduced to raw materials and transformed into new and often different products.
REFUSE	*See* SOLID WASTE.
REFUSE RECLAMATION	The process of converting solid waste to saleable products.

Comment: An example of refuse reclamation is the com-

154

posting of organic solid waste to yield a saleable soil conditioner.

REGION

A geographic area defined by some common feature such as a river basin, housing competition, commutershed, economic activity, or political jurisdiction. *See* HOUSING REGION.

REGIONAL SHOPPING CENTER

See SHOPPING CENTER.

REGULATORY BASE FLOOD

See FLOOD, REGULATORY BASE.

REGULATORY BASE FLOOD DISCHARGE

See FLOOD, REGULATORY BASE DISCHARGE.

REGULATORY FLOODWAY

See FLOODWAY, REGULATORY; FLOODWAY.

REHABILITATION

The upgrading of a building previously in a dilapidated or substandard condition, for human habitation or use.

RELIGIOUS USE

A structure or place in which worship, ceremonies, rituals and education pertaining to a particular system of beliefs are held.

RELOCATE

To move an individual, household, use or building from its original place to another location.

RENT

A periodic payment, made by a tenant, to his landlord for the use of land, buildings, structures or other property, or portions thereof.

REPAIR GARAGE

See GARAGE, REPAIR.

RESEARCH LABORATORY

An establishment or other facility for carrying on investigation in the natural, physical or social sciences, or engineering and development as an extension of investigation with the objective of creating end products.

Comment: Research facilities often include pilot plant operation, and development ordinances usually permit a certain percentage of the floor area (25%, for example) for pilot plant use.

155

RESERVATION

(1) A provision in a deed or other real estate conveyance which preserves a right for the existing owner even if other property rights are transferred; (2) A method of holding land for future public use by designating public areas on a plat, map or site plan as a condition of approval.

RESERVOIR

A pond, lake, tank or basin, natural or man-made, used for the storage, regulation and control of water.

RESIDENCE

A home, abode or place where an individual is actually living at a specific point in time.

Comment: A domicile is the place one intends to maintain as his permanent home. One may have a number of residences but the *permanent* home is called the domicile. *See* DOMICILE.

RESIDENTIAL CLUSTER

An area to be developed as a single entity according to a plan and containing residential housing units which have common or public open space area as an appurtenance. *See* CLUSTER.

RESIDENTIAL DENSITY

The number of dwelling units per acre of residential land.

Comment: The density must be further defined in terms of net or gross. *See* DENSITY.

RESIDENTIAL UNIT

See HOUSEHOLD.

RESORT

A facility for transient guests where the primary attraction is generally recreational features or activities.

RESOURCE RECOVERY

The process of obtaining materials or energy, particularly from solid waste.

REST HOME

See NURSING HOME.

RESTAURANT

An establishment where food and drink is prepared, served and consumed primarily within the principal building. *See* CARRY-OUT RESTAURANT; DRIVE-IN RESTAURANT; FAST-FOOD RESTAURANT; RETAIL FOOD ESTABLISHMENT.

156

RESTORATION	The replication or reconstruction of a building's original architectural features.
	Comment: Restoration is usually used to describe the technique of preserving historic buildings. Rehabilitation, which also accomplishes building upgrading, does not necessarily retain the building's original architectural features. *See* REHABILITATION.
RESTRICTION	A limitation on property which may be created in a property deed, lease, mortgage, through certain zoning or subdivision regulations, or as a condition of approval of an application for development.
RESTRICTIVE COVENANT	A restriction on the use of land usually set forth in the deed.
	Comment: The restrictive covenant usually runs with the land and is binding upon subsequent owners of the property.
RESUBDIVIDE	The further division of lots or the relocation of lot lines of any lot or lots within a subdivision previously made and approved or recorded according to law; or the alteration of any streets or the establishment of any new streets within any such subdivision, but not including conveyances made so as to combine existing lots by deed or other instrument.
RETAIL FOOD ESTABLISHMENT	Any fixed or mobile place or facility at or in which food or drink is offered or prepared for retail sale or for service with or without charge on or at the premises or elsewhere.
	Comment: Agricultural markets, covered dish suppers or similar type of church or nonprofit type institution meal services usually are exempt and fall under the definition of a temporary retail food establishment.
RETAIL SERVICES	Establishments providing services or entertainment, as opposed to products, to the general public, including eating and drinking places, hotels and motels, finance, real estate and insurance, personal services, motion pictures, amusement and recreation services, health, educational and social services, museums and galleries.
	Comment: Retail service attempts to break down the general category of services into those suitable for small-scale or less intensive business zones. For a different approach, *see* SERVICES or PERSONAL SERVICES.

157

RETAIL TRADE

Establishments engaged in selling goods or merchandise to the general public for personal or household consumption and rendering services incidental to the sale of such goods.

Comment: Some of the important characteristics of retail trade establishments are: (1) The establishment is usually a place of business and is engaged in activity to attract the general public to buy; (2) The establishment buys and receives as well as sells merchandise; (3) It may process some of the products, but such processing usually is incidental or subordinate to the selling activities; and (4) Retail establishments sell to customers for their own personal or household use.

Lumber yards, paint, glass and wallpaper stores usually are included in the retail trade even though a substantial portion of their business may be to contractors. Other establishments classified as retail also may sell to professional offices and other business establishments. These products are office supplies, typewriters, etc.

Another important characteristic of a retail trade establishment is that it buys goods for resale. A farmer, for example, selling goods grown on his own property, would not be classified as a retailer. A farmstand which brings in goods from other farmers would be classified as a retail outlet. Eating and drinking places also may be classified as retail establishments although more often they are classified under retail services.

RETAINING WALL

A structure constructed to hold back or support an earthen bank.

RETENTION BASIN

A pond, pool or basin used for the permanent storage of water runoff.

Comment: Retention basins differ from detention basins in that the latter are temporary storage areas. Retention basins may offer potential for water recreation since the water remains. Both types of basins may provide for controlled release of the water.

RETIREMENT COMMUNITIES

Planned developments designed to meet the needs of, and exclusively for, the residences of senior citizens.

Comment: The minimum age varies but it usually is established at around 50 years of age.

158

 **RETURN**

The line between the mean high water line and the seaward extension of a permitted structure, such as a bulkhead.

 **REUSE**

A use for an existing building or parcel of land other than for which it was originally intended.

Comment: Reuse alternatives have been used in historic preservation where the exterior, and sometimes interior, features of a structure have been retained while the building is used for a purpose other than that for which it was constructed originally.

 REVERBERATION

The persistence of sound in an enclosed or confined space after the sound source has stopped.

 REVERSE FRONTAGE

See LOT, REVERSE FRONTAGE.

 REVERSE OSMOSIS

An advanced method of waste treatment relying on a semipermeable membrane to separate waters from pollutants.

 **REVERSION**

The return of real estate to its original owner or owner's heirs.

Comment: Many donations of land to a municipality specify that if the property is not used for the purpose for which it was donated, it reverts back to the owner. Another example is a street which may have been platted but never constructed and which is subsequently abandoned by the municipality. The unused right-of-way reverts back to abutting land owners.

REZONE

To change the zoning classification of particular lots or parcels of land.

RIDGE LINE

The intersection of two roof surfaces forming the highest horizontal line of the roof. *See Figure 28.*

RIDING ACADEMY

An establishment where horses are boarded and cared for and where instruction in riding, jumping and showing is offered and the general public may, for a fee, hire horses for riding.

159

 **RIGHT OF ACCESS**   The legal authority to enter or leave a property.

Comment: In privately owned property, right of access usually means access to a public road. In rented property, right of access also could mean the landlord's right to enter the property to make repairs.

 **RIGHT-OF-WAY**   (1) A strip of land acquired by reservation, dedication, forced dedication, prescription or condemnation and intended to be occupied or occupied by a road, crosswalk, railroad, electric transmission lines, oil or gas pipeline, water line, sanitary storm sewer and other similar uses; (2) Generally, the right of one to pass over the property of another. *See Figure 1.*

 **RIGHT-OF-WAY LINES**   The lines that form the boundaries of a right-of-way. *See Figure 1.*

RINGELMANN CHART   A device used to measure the opacity of smoke emitted from stacks and other sources.

Comment: The chart has a series of illustrations ranging from light gray to black. The shades of gray simulate various smoke densities and are assigned numbers ranging from one to five. Ringelmann No. 1 is equivalent to 20% dense; No. 5 is 100% dense. Ringelmann charts are used in the setting and enforcement of emission standards.

RIPARIAN GRANT   The grant by the state of the lands below the mean high water line usually beginning at the shore and extending outward to the center of the stream or some predetermined line.

Comment: Riparian grants mainly affect tidal waters; those varied by tides.

RIPARIAN LAND   Land that is traversed or bounded by a natural watercourse or adjoining tidal lands.

RIPARIAN RIGHTS   Rights of a land owner to the water on or bordering his property, including the right to make use of such waters and to prevent diversion or misuse of upstream water.

RIVER   A natural stream of water, of greater volume than a creek, flowing in a more or less permanent bed or channel, between defined banks or walls, with a current which either may be continuous in one direction or affected by the ebb and flow of the tide.

RIVER BASIN The total area drained by a river and its tributaries. *See* BASIN.

ROAD *See* STREET.

ROD A lineal measure equal to 16.5 feet or 5.5 yards.

Comment: This surveyor's measure is no longer in use. Four rods equal one chain. Ten chains by ten chains equals 10 acres. *See* CHAIN.

ROOF The outside top covering of a building. *See Figure 28.*

ROOF, FLAT A roof which is not pitched and the surface of which is parallel to the ground. *See Figure 28.*

ROOF, GABLE A ridged roof forming a gable at both ends of the building. *See Figure 28.*

ROOF, GAMBREL A gabled roof with two slopes on each side, the lower steeper than the upper. *See Figure 28.*

ROOF, HIP A roof with sloping ends and sides. *See Figure 28.*

ROOF, MANSARD A roof with two slopes on each of four sides, the lower steeper than the upper. *See Figure 28*

Comment: In current use the upper slope may be flat.

ROOF, SHED A roof with one slope. *See Figure 28.*

ROOMER *See* BOARDER.

ROOMING HOUSE *See* BOARDING HOUSE.

ROOMING UNIT Any habitable room or group of rooms forming a single habitable unit, used or intended to be used for living and sleeping, but not for cooking or eating.

ROW HOUSE *See* DWELLING, TOWNHOUSE.

161

 **RUBBISH**

A general term for solid waste, excluding food waste and ashes, taken from residences, commercial establishments and institutions.

 **RUN WITH THE LAND**

A covenant or restriction to the use of land contained in a deed and binding on the present and all future owners of the property.

Comment: A promise never to divide the land into more lots is incorporated in a deed and the prohibition against subdivision is said to "run with the land" since future owners also are bound by the restriction.

 **RUNOFF**

The portion of rainfall, melted snow or irrigation water that flows across ground surface and eventually is returned to streams. *See Figure 31.*

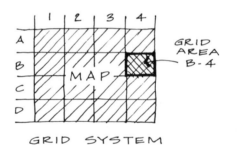 **RURAL AREA**

A sparsely developed area, with a population density of less than 100 persons per acre, where the land is undeveloped or primarily used for agricultural purposes.

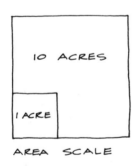

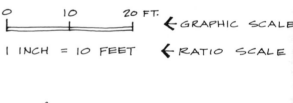

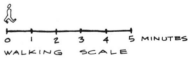

Figure 24

S

 **SALE**

The exchange of goods or property for money or some other consideration.

 **SALINE LAND**

Land with a high salt content that makes it unsuitable for agricultural cultivation.

SALINITY

The degree of salt in water.

SALT WATER INTRUSION

The invasion of salt water into a body of fresh water, occurring in either surface or groundwater bodies. *See Figure 31.*

SALVAGE

The utilization of waste materials.

SAMPLING

A statistical technique of selecting a proportion of a group and examining it as representative of the whole.

SAND PIT

A surface mine or excavation used for the removal of sand, gravel, or fill dirt for sale or for use off-tract. *See* GRAVEL PIT; QUARRY.

SANITARY LAND FILL

A site for solid waste disposal.

Comment: The term implies that the land fill operator follows "sanitary" landfilling techniques.

SANITARY LANDFILLING

A planned method of solid waste disposal in which the solid waste is spread in thin layers, compacted to the smallest practical volume, and covered with soil at the end of each working day.

SANITARY SEWAGE

Any liquid waste containing animal or vegetable matter in suspension or solution, or the water-carried waste resulting from the discharge of water closets, laundry tubs, washing machines, sinks, dishwashers, or any other source of water-carried waste of human origin or containing putrescible material.

SANITARY SEWERS

Pipes that carry only domestic or commercial sewage and into which storm, surface and ground waters are not intentionally admitted. *See* SEWER; COMBINED SEWERS.

163

SANITATION

The control of all the factors in the physical environment that exercise or can exercise a deleterious effect on human physical development, health and survival.

SANITORIUM

A hospital used for treating chronic and usually long-term illness.

SCALE

The relationship between distances on a map and actual ground distances. *See Figure 24.*

Comment: Map scale usually is represented by a graphic scale (by a visual bar) or by a ratio (or representational fraction) such as 1 inch (on the map) = 1 mile (on the ground). Since maps are often enlarged or reduced photographically, the bar scale that is not affected by map enlargement or reduction should be used. *See* AREA SCALE.

SCATTERED SITE HOUSING

New or rehabilitated subsidized dwellings located in substantially built up areas.

Comment: The theory behind scattered site housing is to locate subsidized units throughout established neighborhoods as opposed to concentrating the units in one area. *See* ODD-LOT DEVELOPMENT.

SCENIC AREA

An open area the natural features of which are visually significant or geologically or botanically unique.

SCENIC EASEMENT

An easement the purpose of which is to limit development in order to preserve a view or scenic area. *See* EASEMENT, CONSERVATION.

SCHOOL

Any building or part thereof which is designed, constructed or used for educational or instruction in any branch of knowledge.

Comment: The above definition includes business schools and trade schools, as well as academic institutions. Local ordinances can further define the kinds of schools that might be allowed in a particular neighborhood, for example, elementary and secondary schools. Regulations affecting schools have to be applied uniformly to private and public schools. *See Roman Catholic Diocese of Newark* v. *Borough of Ho-Ho-Kus,* 202 A.2d 161 (1964).

 **SCHOOL DISTRICT**

A district that serves as a unit for state financing and administration of elementary and secondary schools.

SCHOOL, ELEMENTARY

Any school licensed by the State and which meets the State requirements for elementary education.

SCHOOL, PAROCHIAL

A school supported and controlled by a church or religious organization. *See* SCHOOL, PRIVATE.

SCHOOL, PRIVATE

Any building or group of buildings the use of which meets state requirements for primary, secondary or higher education and which use does not secure the major part of its funding from any governmental agency.

SCHOOL, SECONDARY

Any school licensed by the State and which is authorized to award diplomas for secondary education.

SCHOOL, VOCATIONAL

See VOCATIONAL SCHOOL.

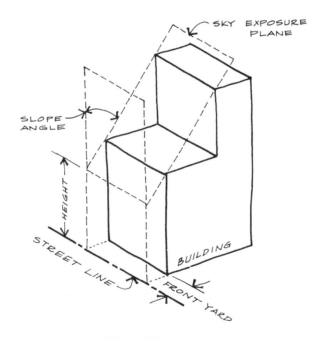

Figure 25

SCRAP

Discarded or rejected materials that result from manufacturing or fabricating operations.

165

SCREENING

(1) A method of visually shielding or obscuring one abutting or nearby structure or use from another by fencing, walls, berms or densely planted vegetation; (2) The removal of relatively coarse floating and/or suspended solids by straining through racks or screens.

SCRUBBER

An air pollution control device that uses a liquid spray to remove pollutants from a gas stream by absorption or chemical reaction.

SEA LEVEL

A reference or datum mark measuring land elevation using the level of the ocean between high and low tides.

SEA SHORE

The area where the land meets the sea or ocean.

SEASONAL DWELLING UNIT

A dwelling unit that lacks one or more of the basic amenities or utilities required for all year or all weather occupancy.

Comment: In resort or seashore areas, municipalities may grant certificates of occupancy for dwelling units which place limits on their occupancy during certain periods of time. For example, houses that lack heating would not be certified for use during winter months.

SEASONAL STRUCTURE

A temporary covering erected over a recreational amenity, such as a swimming pool or tennis court, for the purpose of extending its use to cold weather months or inclement conditions.

SEASONAL USE

A use carried on for only a part of the year such as outdoor swimming during the summer months or skiing during the winter months.

SEAWALL

A wall or embankment that acts as a breakwater and is used to prevent beach erosion.

SECOND HOME COMMUNITY

A development consisting primarily of vacation homes or resort residences.

SECONDARY TREATMENT

Waste water treatment beyond the primary stage, in which bacteria consume the organic parts of the wastes.

Comment: This biochemical action is accomplished by use of trickling filters or the activated sludge process. Effective secondary treatment removes virtually all floating and settleable solids and approximately 90% of both BOD and suspended solids. Customarily, disin-

166

fection by chlorination is the final stage of the secondary treatment process.

SECTION OF LAND

640 acres, 1 square mile (1/36 of a township).

SEDIMENT

Deposited silt that is being or has been moved by water or ice, wind, gravity or other means of erosion. *See* SILT.

SEDIMENT BASIN

A barrier or dam built across a waterway or at suitable locations to retain sediment.

SEDIMENTATION

(1) The depositing of earth or soil that has been transported from its site of origin by water, ice, wind, gravity or other natural means as a product of erosion; (2) In waste water treatment, the settling out of solids by gravity.

SEDIMENTATION TANKS

In waste water treatment, tanks where the solids are allowed to settle or to float as scum.

Comment: Scum is skimmed off; settled solids are pumped to incinerators, digesters, filters or other means of disposal.

SEEPAGE

Water that flows through the soil.

SEEPAGE PIT

A covered pit with open, jointed lining through which septic tank effluent or laundry waste may seep or leach into the surrounding soil.

SEMIDETACHED

See DWELLING, SEMIDETACHED.

SEMIFINISHED PRODUCT

The end result of a manufacturing process which will become a raw material for an establishment engaged in further manufacturing.

Comment: The above definition, from the *Standard Industrial Classification Manual,* includes the following illustration of a semifinished product. The product of the copper smelter is the raw material used in electrolytic refineries; refined copper is the raw material used by copper wire mills; and copper wire is the raw material used by electrical equipment manufacturers. In each case, the product serves as a raw material for subsequent manufacturing activities.

167

SENIOR CITIZEN HOUSING   *See* HOUSING FOR THE ELDERLY.

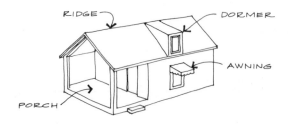

Figure 26

SEPTIC SYSTEM   An underground system with a septic tank used for the decomposition of domestic wastes. *See Figure 30.*

Comment: Bacteria in the wastes decompose the organic matter, and the sludge settles to the bottom. The effluent flows through drains into the ground. Sludge is pumped out at regular intervals.

SEPTIC TANK   A water-tight receptacle that receives the discharge of sewage from a building, sewer or part thereof, and is designed and constructed so as to permit settling of solids from this liquid, digestion of the organic matter, and discharge of the liquid portion into a disposal area. *See Figure 30.*

SERVICE STATION   *See* AUTOMOBILE SERVICE STATION.

SERVICES   Establishments primarily engaged in providing services for individuals, business and government establishments and other organizations; including hotels and other lodging places; establishments providing personal, business, repair and amusement services; health, legal, engineering, and other professional services; educational institutions; membership organizations, and other miscellaneous services. *See* BUSINESS SERVICES; PERSONAL SERVICES; RETAIL SERVICES; SOCIAL SERVICES.

Comment: The above definition includes all types of services and would be appropriate for intensive commercial and retail districts such as found in the central business district of an urban area. Development ordinances may include different types of services appropriate for neighborhood or local business areas.

168

SETBACK

The distance between the street right-of-way line and the front line of a building or any projection thereof, excluding uncovered steps. *See Figure 20.*

Comment: Where the setback is narrow, as in an urban area, even steps may be required to be behind the setback.

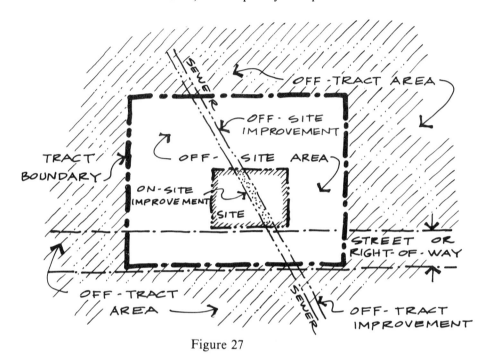

Figure 27

 SETBACK LINE

That line that is the required minimum distance from the street right-of-way line or any other lot line that establishes the area within which the principal structure must be erected or placed. *See* BUILDING LINE. *See Figure 20.*

 **SETTLEABLE SOLIDS**

Bits of debris and fine matter heavy enough to settle out of waste water.

 **SETTLING CHAMBER**

In air pollution control, a device used to reduce the velocity of flue gases, usually by means of baffles, promoting the settling of fly ash.

 **SETTLING TANK**

In waste water treatment, a tank or basin in which settleable solids are removed by gravity.

 **SEWAGE**

The total of organic waste and waste water generated by residential and industrial and commercial establishments.

169

 **SEWER**

Any pipe or conduit used to collect and carry away sewage or storm water runoff from the generating source to treatment plants or receiving streams.

Comment: A sewer that conveys household, commercial and industrial sewage is called a sanitary sewer; if it transports runoff from rain or snow, it is a storm sewer. If storm water runoff and sewage are transported in the same system, then it is a combined sewer.

 SEWER SYSTEM AND TREATMENT

Man-made devices for the collection, treatment and disposal of sewage. *See* COMBINED SEWERS; INTERCEPTOR SEWER; LATERAL SEWERS; OUTFALL; PACKAGE PLANT; PRETREATMENT; PRIMARY TREATMENT; SANITARY SEWAGE; SANITARY SEWERS; SECONDARY TREATMENT; SEPTIC SYSTEM; SEWER; SEWERAGE; TERTIARY TREATMENT.

 **SEWERAGE**

(1) All effluent carried by sewers whether it is sanitary sewage, industrial wastes or storm water runoff; (2) The entire system of sewage collection, treatment and disposal.

 SHELTERED CARE FACILITY

See BOARDING HOME FOR SHELTERED CARE.

SHIELD

A wall that protects workers from harmful radiation released by radioactive materials.

SHOPPING CENTER

A group of commercial establishments planned, constructed and managed as a total entity with customer and employee parking provided on-site, provision for goods delivery separated from customer access, aesthetic considerations and protection from the elements.

Comment: Shopping centers are further defined by size and the area their shoppers come from: (1) A *super regional center* includes retail, office, and service uses, occupies over 100 acres, has four or more anchor stores and contains over one million square feet of gross leasable space; (2) A *regional shopping center* contains a wide range of retail and service establishments, occupies 50 to 100 acres of land, has at least one or more anchor stores, and contains over 400,000 square feet of gross leasable

170

space. It draws its clientele from as much as a 45-minute drive away; (3) *Community shopping centers* will feature a junior department store with approximately 150,000 square feet of gross leasable area, and have a site area of 10 to 25 acres. Its clientele will come a radius of a 10-minute drive from the center; (4) *Neighborhood shopping centers* generally sell goods necessary to meet daily needs, occupies up to 10 acres, has up to 100,000 square feet of gross leasable area, and draws it clientele from a 5-minute radius from the center. *See* MINI-MALL; SPECIALITY SHOPPING CENTER.

 SIDE YARD   *See* YARD, SIDE.

SIDEWALK   A paved, surfaced or leveled area, paralleling and usually separated from the street, used as a pedestrian walkway.

SIGHT TRIANGLE   A triangular shaped portion of land established at street intersections in which nothing is erected, placed, planted or allowed to grow in such a manner as to limit or obstruct the sight distance of motorists entering or leaving the intersection. *See Figure 1.*

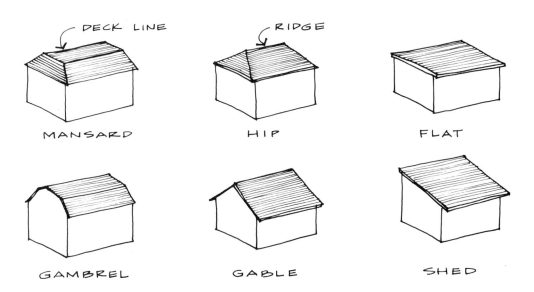

ROOF TYPES

MANSARD · HIP · FLAT · GAMBREL · GABLE · SHED

Figure 28

171

| | | **SIGN** | Any object, device, display or structure, or part thereof, situated outdoors or indoors, which is used to advertise, identify, display, direct or attract attention to an object, person, institution, organization, business, product, service, event or location by any means, including words, letters, figures, design, symbols, fixtures, colors, illumination or projected images. |

Comment: Ordinances usually exclude from the definition of signs national or state flags, window displays, graffiti, athletic scoreboards, or the official announcements or signs of government.

SIGN, ANIMATED OR MOVING

Any sign or part of a sign which changes physical position by any movement or rotation or which gives the visual impression of such movement or rotation.

SIGN AREA

The entire face of a sign including the advertising surface and any framing, trim or molding, but not including the supporting structure.

SIGN, AWNING, CANOPY OR MARQUEE

A sign that is mounted or painted on, or attached to, an awning, canopy, or marquee that is otherwise permitted by ordinance. *See Figure 29.*

Comment: Regulations usually specify that the sign shall not project above, below or beyond the awning, canopy or marquee.

SIGN, BILLBOARD

A sign which directs attention to a business, commodity, service or entertainment conducted, sold or offered at a location other than the premises on which the sign is located.

SIGN, BULLETIN BOARD

A sign which identifies an institution or organization on the premises of which it is located and which contains the name of the institution or organization, the names of individuals connected with it, and general announcements of events or activities occurring at the institution or similar messages.

SIGN, BUSINESS

A sign which directs attention to a business or profession conducted, or to a commodity or service sold, offered or manufactured, or to an entertainment offered on the premises where the sign is located.

SIGN, CONSTRUCTION	A temporary sign erected on the premises on which construction is taking place, during the period of such construction, indicating the names of the architects, engineers, landscape architects, contractors or similar artisans, and the owners, financial supporters, sponsors, and similar individuals or firms having a role or interest with respect to the structure or project.
SIGN, DIRECTIONAL	Signs limited to directional messages, principally for pedestrian or vehicular traffic, such as "one-way," "entrance," and "exit."
SIGN, FACADE	*See* SIGN WALL.
SIGN, FACE	The area or display surface used for the message.
SIGN, FLASHING	Any directly or indirectly illuminated sign which exhibits changing natural or artificial light or color effects by any means whatsoever.
SIGN, FREE STANDING	Any nonmovable sign not affixed to a building.
SIGN, GOVERNMENTAL	A sign erected and maintained pursuant to and in discharge of any governmental functions, or required by law, ordinance or other governmental regulation.
SIGN, GROUND	Any sign, other than a pole sign, placed upon or supported by the ground independent of any other structure. *See Figure 29.*
SIGN, HOLIDAY DECORATION	Temporary signs, in the nature of decorations, clearly incidental to and customarily and commonly associated with any national, local or religious holiday.
SIGN, HOME OCCUPATION	A sign containing only the name and occupation of a permitted home occupation.
SIGN, IDENTIFICATION	A sign giving the nature, logo, trademark or other identifying symbol; address; or any combination of the name, symbol and address of a building, business, development or establishment on the premises where it is located.
SIGN, ILLUMINATED	A sign lighted by or exposed to artificial lighting either by lights on or in the sign or directed towards the sign.

173

SIGN, MEMORIAL

A sign, tablet or plaque memorializing a person, event, structure or site.

SIGN, NAME PLATE

A sign, located on the premises, giving the name or address, or both, of the owner or occupant of a building or premises.

SIGN, OFF-PREMISE

See SIGN, BILLBOARD.

SIGN, ON-SITE INFORMATIONAL

A sign commonly associated with, and not limited to, information and directions necessary or convenient for visitors coming on the property, including signs marking entrances and exits, parking areas, circulation direction, rest rooms, and pick-up and delivery areas.

SIGN, POLE

A sign that is mounted on a free standing pole or other support so that the bottom edge of the sign face is six feet or more above grade. *See Figure 29.*

SIGN, POLITICAL

A temporary sign announcing or supporting political candidates or issues in connection with any national, state or local election.

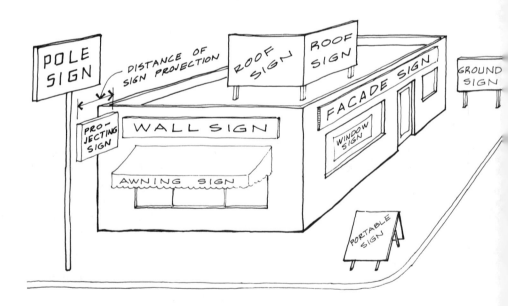

SIGN TYPES

Figure 29

SIGN, PORTABLE	A sign that is not permanent, affixed to a building, structure or the ground. *See Figure 29.*
SIGN, PRIVATE SALE OR EVENT	A temporary sign advertising private sales of personal property such as "house sales," "garage sales," "rummage sales" and the like or private not-for-profit events such as picnics, carnivals, bazaars, game nights, art fairs, craft shows and Christmas tree sales.
SIGN, PROJECTING	A sign that is wholly or partly dependent upon a building for support and which projects more than 12 inches from such building. *See Figure 29.*
SIGN, REAL ESTATE	A sign pertaining to the sale or lease of the premises, or a portion of the premises, on which the sign is located.
SIGN, ROOF	A sign that is mounted on the roof of a building or which is wholly dependent upon a building for support and which projects above the point of a building with a flat roof, the eave line of a building with a gambrel, gable or hip roof or the deck line of a building with a mansard roof. *See Figure 29.*
SIGN, TEMPORARY	A sign or advertising display constructed of cloth, canvas, fabric, plywood or other light material and designed or intended to be displayed for a short period of time.
SIGN, WALL	A sign fastened to or painted on the wall of a building or structure in such a manner that the wall becomes the supporting structure for, or forms the background surface of the sign and which does not project more than 12 inches from such building or structure. *See Figure 29.*
SIGN, WARNING	Signs limited to messages of warning, danger or caution.
SIGN, WINDOW	A sign that is applied or attached to the exterior or interior of a window or located in such manner within a building that it can be seen from the exterior of the structure through a window. *See Figure 29.*
SILT	Finely divided particles of soil or rock, often carried in cloudy suspension in water and eventually deposited as sediment.
SILVICULTURE	The development and/or maintenance of a forest or wooded preserve.

175

SINGLE OWNERSHIP

Ownership by one or more persons in any form of ownership of a lot or lots partially or entirely in the same ownership.

Comment: The definition of single ownership becomes important since most ordinances permit the development of undersized isolated lots providing they are in single ownership. *See* ISOLATED LOT.

SINGLE-FAMILY DWELLING

See DWELLING, SINGLE-FAMILY.

SINKING

A method of controlling oil spills that employs an agent to entrap oil droplets and sink them to the bottom of the body of water.

SITE

Any plot or parcel of land or combination of contiguous lots or parcels of land. *See Figure 27.*

SITE PLAN

The development plan for one or more lots on which is shown the existing and proposed conditions of the lot including: topography, vegetation, drainage, floodplains, marshes and waterways; open spaces, walkways, means of ingress and egress, utility services, landscaping, structures and signs, lighting, and screening devices; any other information that reasonably may be required in order that an informed decision can be made by the approving authority.

Comment: Many ordinances classify small site plans (5 acres in rural areas; less in urban areas) as minor site plans and relieve the applicant of some of the submission requirements.

SKATEBOARD PARK

A building, structure or open area containing or developed with slopes, hills, passageways and other challenges where people using skateboards may practice the sport for a fee; rental or sale of skateboards and related equipment may be included.

SKETCH PLAN

See PLAT, SKETCH.

SKI AREA

An area developed for snow skiing, with trails and lifts, and including ski rental and sales, instruction, and eating facilities.

SKI RESORT

A ski area which also includes sales, rental and service of related equipment and accessories, eating places, residences and hotels and motels. *See* SKI AREA.

176

■ SKILLED NURSING HOME   *See* EXTENDED CARE FACILITY.

▲ SKIMMING   The mechanical removal of oil or scum from the surface of water.

■ ▬ SKY EXPOSURE PLANE   A theoretical plane beginning at a lot line or directly above a street line at a height set forth in the ordinance, and rising over a slope determined by an acute angle measured down from the vertical as set forth in the ordinance. *See Figure 25.*

■▶▬▲ SLOPE   The degree of deviation of a surface from the horizontal, usually expressed in percent or degrees. *See* GRADE. *See Figure 16.*

▲ SLUDGE   Solids removed from sewage during waste water treatment and then disposed of by incineration, dumping or burial.

■▶▬▲ SLUM   *See* BLIGHTED AREA.

▲ SMOG   Generally used as an equivalent of air pollution, particularly associated with oxidants.

▲ SMOKE   Solid particles generated as a result of the incomplete combustion of materials containing carbon.

■ SOCIAL SERVICES   Establishments providing assistance and aid to those persons requiring counseling for psychological problems, employment, learning disabilities, and physical disabilities.

Comment: This major group also includes organizations soliciting funds for these and related services. They also include child day-care services, nurseries as well as residential care, and special categories for persons with limited ability for self-care but for whom medical care is not a major element.

■▶▬▲ SOIL   All unconsolidated mineral and organic material of whatever origin that overlies bedrock and can be readily excavated.

■▶▬▲ SOIL CONDITIONER   A biologically stable organic material such as humus or compost that makes soil more amenable to the passage of water and to the distribution of fertilizing material, providing a better medium for necessary soil bacteria growth.

177

 **SOIL CONSERVATION DISTRICT**

A governmental subdivision that provides advice to communities, agencies and individuals within its jurisdiction, and reviews development proposals, for soil erosion and sedimentation control measures.

 **SOIL ENGINEER**

A professional engineer who is qualified by education and experience to practice applied soil mechanics and foundation engineering.

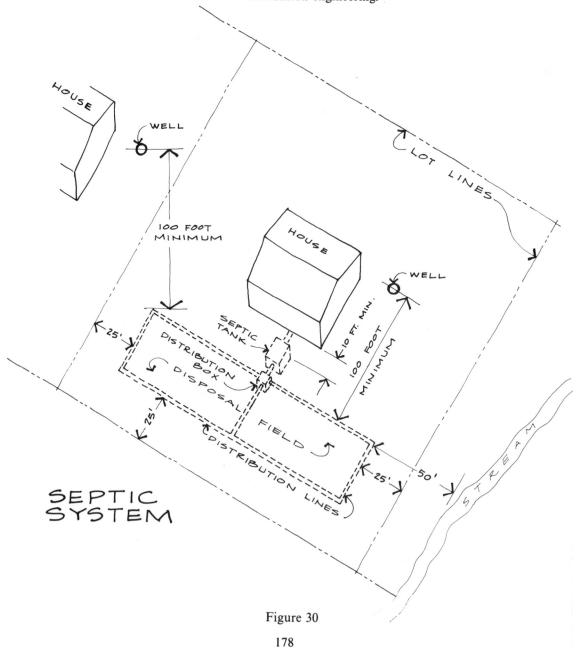

Figure 30

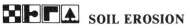 **SOIL EROSION**

See EROSION.

 SOIL EROSION AND SEDIMENT CONTROL PLAN

A plan that indicates necessary land treatment measures, including a schedule for installation, which will effectively minimize soil erosion and sedimentation.

 **SOIL MAP**

A map prepared by the Soil Conservation Service of the Department of Agriculture, indicating the following soil characteristics: slope, depth to seasonal high water, depth to bedrock, permeability, natural drainage class, stoniness, and flood and stream overflow hazard.

 **SOLAR ACCESS**

A property owner's right to have the sunlight shine on his land.

Comment: The enforcement of this right is through the zoning ordinance which establishes height and setback requirements. Applicants may be asked to present sun shadow diagrams to permit an agency to determine if solar access will be impaired.

 **SOLAR ENERGY SYSTEM**

A complete design or assembly consisting of a solar energy collector, an energy storage facility (where used), and components for the distribution of transformed energy.

Comment: Passive solar energy systems are usually included in this definition. Some judgment is required, however, when the passive systems are used for structural and recreational purposes. When they become predominantly structural or recreational, then they are usually excluded from the definition.

 **SOLAR SKYSPACE**

The space between a solar energy collector and the sun which must be free of obstructions that shade the collector to an extent which precludes its cost-effective operation.

Comment: Increasingly, planners will be asked to develop zoning requirements which protect the solar skyspace. It can be done through minimum setback requirements and sky exposure planes. Site plan review might also require a shadow analysis to ascertain whether or not any proposed tree plantings, landscaping or structures will block off solar collectors. For single-family and two-family homes which are usually excluded from site plan review, the construction code official or building

179

inspector should be given guidelines as to what may be permitted and how close to the structure in order to assure a functioning solar collector.

 **SOLAR SKYSPACE EASEMENT**

A right, expressed as an easement, covenant, condition, or other property interest in any deed or other instrument executed by or on behalf of any landowner, which protects the solar skyspace of an actual, proposed, or designated solar energy collector at a described location by forbidding or limiting activities or land uses that interfere with access to solar energy.

Comment: The solar skyspace must be described either as the three-dimensional space in which obstruction is prohibited or limited, or as the times of day in which direct sunlight to the solar collector may not be obstructed, or as a combination of the two methods.

SOLID WASTE

Unwanted or discarded material, including garbage with insufficient liquid content to be free flowing.

Comment: Solid waste may be categorized as follows: (1) Agricultural—Solid waste that results from the raising and slaughtering of animals, and the processing of animal products and orchard and field crops; (2) Commercial—Waste generated by stores, offices and other activities that do not actually turn out a product; (3) Industrial—Waste that results from industrial processes and manufacturing; (4) Institutional—Waste originating from educational, health care and research facilities; (5) Municipal—Residential and commercial solid waste generated within a community; (6) Pesticide—The residue from the manufacturing, handling, or use of chemicals intended for killing plant and animal pests; (7) Residential—Waste that normally originates in a residential environment, sometimes called domestic solid waste.

SOLID WASTE DISPOSAL

The ultimate disposition of solid waste that cannot be salvaged or recycled.

SOLID WASTE MANAGEMENT

A planned program providing for the collection, storage, and disposal of solid waste including, where appropriate, recycling and recovery.

SONIC BOOM

The sound produced by the shock waves of a vehicle exceeding the speed of sound through the atmosphere.

180

■ SOOT

Agglomerations of tar-impregnated carbon particles that form when carbonaceous-material does not undergo complete combustion.

■ SORORITY HOUSE

See FRATERNITY HOUSE.

■ SPECIAL ASSESSMENT

A fee levied by a local authority for the financing of a local improvement that is primarily of benefit to the landowners who must pay the assessment.

■ SPECIAL DISTRICT

A district created by act, petition or vote of the residents for a specific purpose with the power to levy taxes.

■ SPECIAL EXCEPTION USE

See CONDITIONAL USE.

■ SPECIAL USE PERMIT

A permit issued by the proper governmental authority which must be acquired before a special exception use can be constructed. *See* CONDITIONAL USE PERMIT.

■ SPECIALTY FOOD STORE

A retail store specializing in a specific type or class of foods such as an appetizer store, bakery, butcher, delicatessen, fish, gourmet and similar foods.

■ SPECIALTY SHOPPING CENTER

A shopping center whose shops cater to a specific market and are linked together by an architectural, historical or geographic theme or by a commonality of goods and services. Also known as a theme or fashion center. *See* MINI-MALL; SHOPPING CENTER.

■ SPECIFICATIONS

Detailed instructions which designate the quality and quantity of materials and workmanship expected in the construction of a structure.

■ SPEED BUMP

A raised section of a paved surface or roadway designed to interfere with and deter speeding traffic.

Comment: Speed bumps can be hazardous and only are used on private roads and parking areas. They should be well marked with warning signs. Good road and parking area design can usually preclude the need for speed bumps.

■ SPOIL

Dirt or rock that has been removed from its original location or materials that have been dredged from the bottoms of waterways.

SPOT ZONING

Rezoning of a lot or parcel of land to benefit an owner for a use incompatible with surrounding uses and not for the purpose or effect of furthering the comprehensive zoning plan.

Comment: Hagman (*Urban Planning and Land Development Control Law,* West Publishing, page 169), notes that spot zoning per se may not be illegal; it may only be descriptive of a certain set of facts, and consequently neutral with respect to whether it is valid or invalid. He suggests that spot zoning is invalid when all the following factors are present: (1) A small parcel of land is singled out for special and privileged treatment; (2) The singling out is not in the public interest but only for the benefit of the land owner; and (3) The action is not in accord with a comprehensive plan. See *Kozesnik* v. *Twp. of Montgomery,* 24 N.J. 154, 131 A2 1 (1957); *Borough of Cresskill* v. *Borough of Dumont,* 15 N.J. 238, 104 A2d 441 (1954); and *Jones* v. *Zoning Board of Adjustment of Long Beach Twp.,* 32 N.J. Super 397, 108 498 (1954).

SQUARE

A public open space in a developed area. *See* COURT; PLAZA.

SQUATTER

A person who settles on land without the permission of the owner.

STABILIZATION

The process of converting active organic matter in sewage sludge or solid wastes into inert, harmless material.

STABLE

A structure that is used for the shelter or care of horses and cattle.

STACK

A smokestack; a vertical pipe or flue designed to exhaust gases and suspended particulate matter.

STADIUM

A large open or enclosed place used for games and major events and partly or completely surrounded by tiers of seats for spectators.

STALL

The parking space into which vehicles park. *See Figure 2.*

Comment: The size of stalls vary. The typical automobile stall is 9′ X 20′. However, where there is large turnover, such as in a shopping center, a 10′ X 20′ space may be appropriate. In addition, the wider stall will permit easier vehicular access for shoppers burdened with packages. In low turnover situations, an 8½' X 20' stall may suffice. If spaces are assigned, then compact car parking can be as small as 7' X 17'. Where vehicles can overhang a curb, the stall depth can be reduced by 2 feet. *See* PARKING SPACE.

 **STANDARD METROPOLITAN STATISTICAL AREA (SMSA)**

A county or group of contiguous counties which contains at least one city of 50,000 inhabitants or more, or twin cities of a combined population of at least 50,000.

Comment: Only those contiguous counties that are socially and economically integrated into the central city are included. In New England the SMSAs consist of towns and cities instead of counties.

 **STANDARD OF LIVING**

A measure of the adequacy of necessities and comforts in an individuals daily life in reference to the general populace.

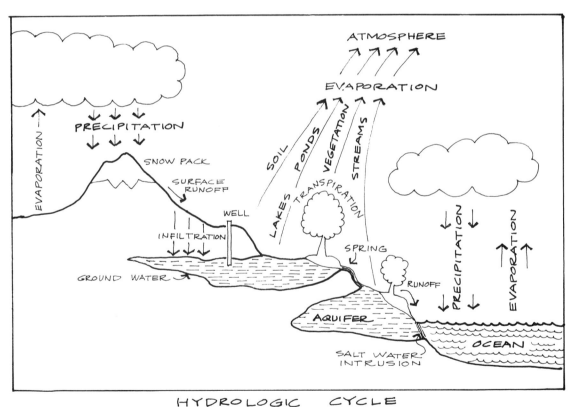

Figure 31

STATIONARY SOURCE

A non-mobile emitter of pollution. *See* AREA SOURCE; POINT SOURCE.

STEEP SLOPE

Land areas where the slope exceeds twenty percent.

Comment: The use of 20% figure is somewhat arbitrary. However, construction on slopes in excess of 20% requires additional safeguards against erosion and other potential problems. Some ordinances reduce the allowable intensity of development as a function of slope in excess of 20%.

STORM SEWER

A conduit that collects and transports runoff.

STORMWATER DETENTION

Any storm drainage technique that retards or detains runoff, such as a detention or retention basin, parking lot storage, rooftop storage, porous pavement, dry wells or any combination thereof. *See* DETENTION BASIN; RETENTION BASIN.

STORY

That portion of a building included between the surface of any floor and the surface of the floor next above it, or if there be no floor above it, then the space between the floor and the ceiling next above it and including those basements used for the principal use. *See Figure 3.*

STORY, HALF

A space under a sloping roof which has the line of intersection of the roof and wall face not more than three feet above the floor level, and in which space the possible floor area with head room of five feet or less occupies at least 40% of the total floor area of the story directly beneath. *See Figure 17.*

STREAM

A watercourse having a source and terminus, banks and channel through which waters flow at least periodically.

Comment: Streams usually empty into lakes, other streams or the ocean, but do not lose their character as a watercourse even though the water may dry up.

STREET

Any vehicular way which: (1) is an existing state, county or municipal roadway; or (2) is shown upon a plat approved pursuant to law; or (3) is approved by other official action; or (4) is shown on a plat duly filed and recorded in the office of the county recording officer prior to the appointment of a planning board and the grant to such board of the power to review plats; and includes the land between the street lines, whether improved or unimproved.

184

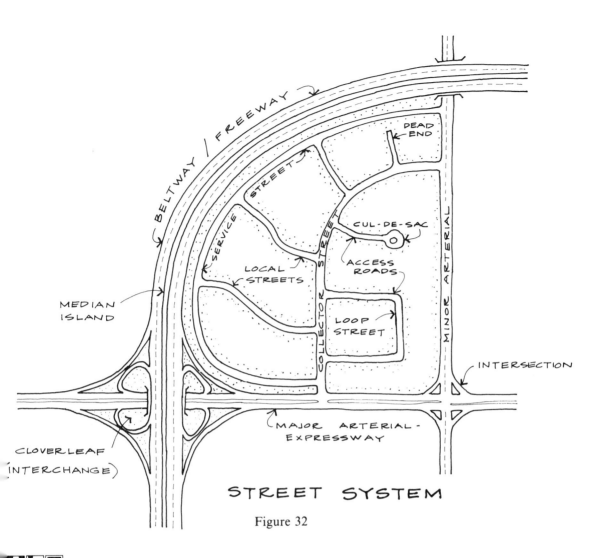

STREET SYSTEM

Figure 32

STREET, COLLECTOR	A street which collects traffic from local streets and connects with minor and major arterials. *See Figure 32.*	
STREET, CUL-DE-SAC	A street with a single common ingress and egress and with a turnaround at the end. *See Figure 32.*	
STREET, DEAD END	A street with a single common ingress and egress. *See Figure 32.*	
STREET, DUAL	A street with opposing lanes separated by a median strip, center island or other form of barrier, which cannot be crossed except at designated locations.	
STREET, EXPRESSWAY	A divided multi-lane major arterial street for through traffic with partial control of access and with grade separations at major intersections. *See Figure 32.*	

185

STREET, FREEWAY	A limited access highway with no grade crossings. *See Figure 32.*
STREET FURNITURE	Man-made, above-ground items that are usually found in street rights-of-way, including benches, kiosks, plants, canopies, shelters and phone booths.
	Comment: Street furniture is distinct from street hardware such as traffic lights, and directional signs.
STREET HARDWARE	Street hardware are mechanical and utility systems within a street right-of-way such as hydrants, manhole covers, traffic lights and signs, utility poles and lines, parking meters and the like.
STREET LINE	*See* RIGHT-OF-WAY LINES.
STREET, LOCAL	A street designed to provide vehicular access to abutting property and to discourage through traffic. *See Figure 32.*
	Comment: Cul-de-sacs and loop streets are both examples of local streets.
STREET, LOOP	A local street which has its only ingress and egress at two points of the same collector street. *See Figure 32.*
STREET, MAJOR ARTERIAL	A street with access control, channelized intersections, restricted parking, and which collects and distributes traffic to and from minor arterials. *See Figure 32.*
STREET, MINOR ARTERIAL	A street with signals at important intersections and stop signs on the side streets, and which collects and distributes traffic to and from collector streets. *See Figure 32.*
STREET, SERVICE	A street running parallel to a freeway or expressway and serving abutting properties. *See Figure 32.*
STRIP DEVELOPMENT	Commercial or retail development, usually one-store deep, that fronts on a major street.
STRIP MINING	A process of recovering ore or fuel deposits by mechanically scraping away the overhanging rock and strata.
	Comment: Strip mining is also known as surface mining.
STRIP ZONING	*See* STRIP DEVELOPMENT.

186

STRUCTURAL ALTERATION	Any change in either the supporting members of a building, such as bearing walls, columns, beams and girders, or in the dimensions or configurations of the roof or exterior walls.
STRUCTURE	A combination of materials to form a construction for use, occupancy, or ornamentation whether installed on, above, or below the surface of land or water.
	Comment: By this definition, all buildings are structures; however, not all structures are buildings. *See* BUILDING.
STUD FARM	A farm where a stallion stands at stud and mares are bred to him, and where breeding, pasturing and foaling may take place.
STUDIO	A building or portion of a building used as a place of work by an artist, photographer, or artisan, or used for radio or television broadcasting.
STUDIO APARTMENT	*See* DWELLING UNIT, EFFICIENCY.
SUBDIVIDER	Any person having an interest in land that is the subject of an application for subdivision. *See* APPLICANT.
SUBDIVISION	The division of a lot, tract or parcel of land into two or more lots, tracts, parcels or other divisions of land for sale, development or lease.
	Comment: Many state enabling laws exclude certain subdivisions from this definition. For example, in New Jersey the following are not considered subdivisions, providing no new streets are created: (1) Divisions of land for agricultural purposes where all resulting parcels are 5 acres or larger in size; (2) Divisions of property by testamentary or intestate provisions; (3) Divisions of property upon court order, including, but not limited to, judgments of foreclosure; and (4) Conveyances so as to combine existing lots by deed or other instrument.
SUBDIVISION, CLUSTER	*See* CLUSTER SUBDIVISION.
SUBDIVISION, CONSOLIDATION	The combining of individual recorded lots to form a single tract in single ownership. *See* ASSEMBLAGE; CONSOLIDATION.

SUBDIVISION, MAJOR		Any subdivision not classified as a minor subdivision.
SUBDIVISION, MINOR		A subdivision of land that does not involve any of the following: (1) The creating of more than the maximum number of lots specifically permitted by ordinance as a minor subdivision; (2) A planned development; (3) Any new street; or (4) The extension of any off-tract improvements.
SUBMERGED LAND		Those lands situated below the mean low water line or all of the lands covered by the mean high water line.
SUBSIDENCE		The gradual sinking of land as a result of natural or man-made causes.
SUBSIDIZED HOUSING		Housing constructed for and occupied by low- or moderate-income families. *See* LOW-INCOME HOUSING; MODERATE-INCOME HOUSING; PUBLIC HOUSING.
SUBSOIL		The layer of soil just below the surface of the ground.
SUBSTANDARD STRUCTURE/ DWELLING		A term used in the 1960 and preceding U.S. Censuses of Housing to indicate a lack of some or all plumbing facilities and/or the presence of physical inadequacies.
SUBSTANTIAL IMPROVEMENT		Any extention, repair, reconstruction, or other improvement of a property, the cost of which equals or exceeds fifty percent of the fair market value of a property either before the improvement is started or if the property has been damaged and is being restored, before the damage occurred. *Comment:* Substantial improvement often is used to define the point where a nonconforming use or structure cannot be repaired. The Federal Insurance Administration also requires floodproofing measures to be installed when a structure in a floodway undergoes "substantial improvement."
SULFUR DIOXIDE (SO$_2$)		A heavy, pungent, colorless gas formed primarily by the combustion of fossil fuels that damage the respiratory tract as well as vegetation and certain materials and considered a major air pollutant.
SUMP		A depression or tank that serves as a drain or receptacle of liquids for salvage or disposal.

SUPERMARKET	A retail establishment primarily selling food as well as other convenience and household goods.
	Comment: Supermarkets usually vary in size from 20,000 square feet to 60,000 square feet and provide parking at a ratio of about 5-6 off-street spaces per 1,000 square feet of gross leasable space.
SURFACE WATER	Water on the earth's surface exposed to the atmosphere as rivers, lakes, streams, the oceans. *See* GROUNDWATER.
SURFACTANT	An agent used in detergents to cause lathering.
	Comment: Composed of several phosphate compounds, surfactants are a source of external enrichment thought to speed the eutrophication of lakes.
SURGICAL CENTER	A facility where outpatients come for simple surgical procedures.
	Comment: Surgical centers are more elaborate than a doctor's office but less equipped or varied in service than a hospital.
SURVEILLANCE SYSTEM	A monitoring system to determine environmental quality.
	Comment: Surveillance systems are established to monitor all pollution and other aspects of progress toward attainment of environmental standards. Surveillance systems identify potential episodes of high pollutant concentrations in time to take preventive action.
SURVEY	The process of precisely ascertaining the area, dimensions and location of a piece of land.
SUSPENDED SOLIDS	Small particles of solid pollutants in sewage that contribute to turbidity and that resist separation by conventional means.
	Comment: The examination of suspended solids and the BOD test constitute the two main determinations for water quality performed at waste water treatment facilities.
SWALE	A depression in the ground which channels runoff.

189

■ **SWIMMING POOL**

A water-filled enclosure, permanently constructed or portable, having a depth of more than eighteen inches below the level of the surrounding land, or an above-surface pool, having a depth of more than thirty inches, designed, used and maintained for swimming and bathing.

Comment: The 18-inch exclusion would be effective in permitting landscaping and other shallow, not-for-swimming pools. The 30-inch height for surface pools marks the usual break between portable and nonportable pools.

■▶▶▲ **SYNDICATE**

A group formed to combine capital or other assets for future investment.

■▶▶▲ **SYNERGISM**

The cooperative action of separate substances so that the total effect is greater than the sum of the effects of the substances acting independently.

T

▲ **TAILINGS**

Second grade or waste material derived when raw material is screened or processed.

 **TAKING**

To take, expropriate, acquire or seize property without compensation. *See* EMINENT DOMAIN; JUST COMPENSATION.

■ **TANK FARM**

An open air facility containing a number of above-ground, large containers for the bulk storage of material in liquid, powder or pellet form.

■ **TAVERN**

An establishment used primarily for the serving of liquor by the drink to the general public and where food or packaged liquors may be served or sold only as accessory to the primary use.

■▶▶▲ **TAX EXEMPT PROPERTY**

Property, which because of its ownership or use, is not subject to property taxation and meets state requirements for tax-exempt status.

Comment: All states have specific requirements that qualify properties for tax exempt status.

TEMPORARY PROTECTION

Stabilization of erosive or sediment producing areas by temporary measures until permanent measures are in place.

TEMPORARY RETAIL FOOD ESTABLISHMENT

A retail food establishment that operates at a fixed location for a temporary period of time in connection with a fair, carnival, circus, public exhibition or similar transitory gathering, including church suppers, picnics or similar organizational meetings, mobile retail food establishments, and agricultural markets.

Comment: Temporary retail food establishments are probably best handled as conditional uses and accessory to the principal permitted use; fair, carnival, etc. Some of the more troublesome temporary retail food establishments are those in mobile van units which park alongside main roads near recreation areas. The permanent food establishments, or those inside the recreation areas, resent the "intruders." If allowed in the ordinance as a conditional use, the temporary establishments could be required to provide off-street parking, keep off the right-of-way, and maintain certain minimum sanitary facilities.

TEMPORARY STRUCTURE

A structure without any foundation or footings and which is removed when the designated time period, activity, or use for which the temporary structure was erected has ceased.

TEMPORARY USE

A use established for a fixed period of time with the intent to discontinue such use upon the expiration of the time period.

Comment: Temporary uses usually do not involve the construction or alteration of any permanent building or structure, although the authorization of the temporary use does not necessarily preclude such construction.

TENANT

An occupant of land or premises who occupies, uses, and enjoys real property for a fixed time, usually through a lease arrangement with the property owner and with the owner's consent.

TENEMENT HOUSE

A multifamily dwelling most commonly associated with low-income families and generally characterized as an aging, often substandard structure.

191

▨	**TENNIS COURT**	An improved area used for playing tennis.
		Comment: Development ordinances should specify in which zones open or enclosed courts are permitted.
▨	**TERMINAL**	(1) A place where transfer between modes of transportation take place; (2) A terminating point where goods are transferred from a truck to a storage area or to other trucks, or picked up by other forms of transportation.
▶▐▔▌▲	**TERRACE**	A level, landscaped and/or surfaced area directly adjacent to a principal building at or within three feet of the finished grade and not covered by a permanent roof.
▶▐▔▌▲	**TERRACING**	An erosion control method that uses small hills and contours on the land surface to control flooding and runoff.
▲	**TERTIARY TREATMENT**	Waste water treatment, beyond the secondary, or biological stage, that includes removal of nutrients such as phosphorus and nitrogen, and a high percentage of suspended solids.
		Comment: Tertiary treatment, also known as advanced waste treatment, produces a high quality effluent.
▨	**THEATER**	A building or part of a building devoted to showing motion pictures, or for dramatic, musical or live performances.
▨	**THEATER, DRIVE-IN**	An open lot with its appurtenant facilities devoted primarily to the showing of motion pictures or theatrical productions on a paid admission basis to patrons seated in automobiles.
▨	**THEME PARK**	An entertainment or amusement facility built around a single theme which may be historical, architectural, or cultural.
▲	**THERMAL POLLUTION**	Degradation of water quality by the introduction of a heated effluent.
		Comment: Thermal pollution is primarily the result of the discharge of cooling waters from industrial processes, particularly from electrical power generation.
▶	**THROUGH LOT**	*See* LOT, THROUGH.

192

▲ **TIDE**	A periodic rise and fall of the surface of ocean waters caused by gravitational pull.
▲ **TIDE LAND**	Land between low and high tide.
▲ **TILLABLE LAND**	Fertile land which can be cultivated.
▲ **TIMBERLAND**	Land covered by harvestable trees and wooded areas.
▲ **TOPOGRAPHIC MAP**	A map of a portion of the earth's surface showing its topography. *See* TOPOGRAPHY.
	Comment: Topographic maps often include natural and man-made features.
▲ **TOPOGRAPHY**	The configuration of a surface area showing relative elevations.
▲ **TOPSOIL**	The original upper layer of soil material to a depth of six inches which is usually darker and richer than the subsoil.
TOT LOT	An improved and equipped play area for small children usually up to elementary school age.
TOURIST HOME	An establishment in a private dwelling that supplies temporary accommodations to overnight guests for a fee.
▲ **TOWN, TOWNSHIP**	(1) A developed community, smaller than a city, and larger than a village; (2) In some states, a description of the form of local government; (3) A unit of territory usually six miles square and containing 36-mile-square sections.
TOWN CENTER	*See* CENTRAL BUSINESS DISTRICT.
TOWNHOUSE	*See* DWELLING, TOWNHOUSE.
▲ **TOXIC POLLUTANTS**	A combination of pollutants including disease-carrying agents which, after discharge and upon exposure, ingestion, inhalation, or assimilation into any organism can cause death or disease, mutations, deformities, or malfunctions in such organisms or their offspring.
▲ **TOXICITY**	The quality or degree of being poisonous or harmful to plant or animal life.

193

▲ TRACE METALS   Metals, usually insoluble, found in small quantities or traces.

◨▸�▲ TRACT   An area, parcel, site, piece of land, or property which is the subject of a development application. *See Figure 27.*

▸ TRACT HOUSE   A dwelling in a residential development containing houses similar in size and appearance.

◨▸か▲ TRAFFIC COUNT   A tabulation of the number of vehicles or pedestrians passing a certain point during a specified period of time.

◨▸か▲ TRAFFIC GENERATOR   A use in a particular geographic area which is likely to attract into the area substantial vehicular or pedestrian traffic.

◨ TRAILER   A structure standing on wheels, towed or hauled by another vehicle and used for short-term human occupancy, carrying materials, goods or objects, or as a temporary office.

Comment: Development ordinances may allow for trailers on work sites to be used as temporary offices. *See* MOBILE HOME and RECREATIONAL VEHICLE.

◨ か TRAILER COURT   *See* MOBILE HOME PARK.

◨▸か TRANSFER OF DEVELOPMENT RIGHTS (TDR)   The removal of the right to develop or build, expressed in dwelling units per acre, from land in one zoning district to land in another district where such transfer is permitted.

Comment: Transfer of development rights, or transfer of development credits, is a relatively new land development control tool used to preserve open space and farmland. Presently, the most common use of this method has been for historic preservation in urban areas.

◨ TRANSITION ZONE   A zoning district permitting transitional uses.

◨ TRANSITIONAL AREA   (1) An area in the process of changing from one use to another or changing from one racial or ethnic occupancy to another; (2) An area which acts as a buffer between two land uses of different intensity.

Comment: A transitional area may be, for example, the land area between a business area along a street frontage

194

and the adjacent residential area. Many development ordinances establish transitional districts which permit either residential or some less intensive commercial use to be located between the two different land uses. The less intensive commercial use might be a small office building or institutional use.

TRANSITIONAL CARE HOME

A facility in which individuals live for a short period while receiving physical, social or psychological therapy and counseling to assist them in overcoming physical or emotional problems.

Comment: The transitional care home is a form of halfway house. Residents do not require segregation from society or require shelter away from their usual residences. Professional therapy and counseling is done on a more intensive basis than permitted by an outpatient status.

TRANSITIONAL CLINIC CARE

A clinic operated as a subordinate use in connection with and on the premises of a transitional care home, solely for providing physical, social and psychological therapy or counseling by qualified personnel whose patients are limited to those who have recently resided in the transitional care home or families of those who are residing in or have recently resided in a transitional care home.

TRANSITIONAL USE

A land use of an intermediate intensity between a more intensive and less intensive use.

Comment: Transitional uses always will include the uses from the less intensive district, usually residences, and carefully selected uses allowed in the more intensive district; the purpose being to preclude the more intensive uses from "creeping" into the less intensive zone. *See* TRANSITIONAL AREA.

TRANSPORTATION SERVICES, ACCESSORY

Establishments furnishing services incidental to transportation, such as forwarding and parking services, and the arranging of passenger or freight transportation.

TRANSPORTATION SERVICES, LOCAL

Establishments primarily engaged in furnishing local and suburban passenger transportation, including taxicabs, passenger transportation charter service, school buses, and terminal and service facilities for motor vehicle passenger transportation.

195

TRAP

A fitting or device so designed and constructed as to provide, when properly vented, a liquid seal which will prevent the back passage of air without materially affecting the flow of sewage or wastewater through it.

TRAVEL TRAILER

A recreation vehicle that is towed by a car or a truck. *See* RECREATIONAL VEHICLE.

TREE HOUSE

A structure built above ground level, using a tree for part of its support and not designed for continuous habitation.

TRICKLING FILTER

A device for the biological or secondary treatment of waste water consisting of a bed of rocks or stones that support bacterial growth and permit sewage to be trickled over the bed, enabling the bacteria to break down organic wastes.

TRIP

A single or one-way vehicle movement either to or from a subject property or study area.

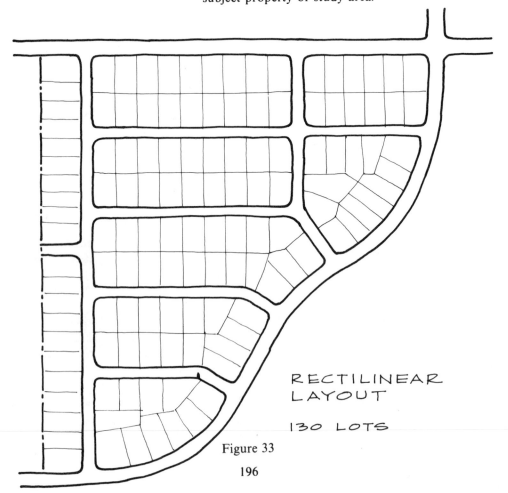

RECTILINEAR
LAYOUT

130 LOTS

Figure 33

TRIP ENDS

The total of trips entering and leaving a specific land use or site over a designated period of time.

TRIP GENERATION

The total number of trip ends produced by a specific land use or activity.

Comment: The most comprehensive data on trip generation is entitled *Trip Generation,* (Maclean, Va.: Institute of Transportation Engineers, 1979). An adaptation of some of the data from *Trip Generation* is illustrated below:

VEHICULAR TRIP GENERATION, BY USE

Land Use	Trip Generation Unit	Trip Volume/ Unit (24-hour weekday)	AM Peak (trips)	PM Peak (trips)
Single Family	Dwelling Unit*	10–15	1.15	1.25
Town House	Dwelling Unit*	6–8	.90	1.00
Garden Apartment	Dwelling Unit*	4–6	.60	.70
High Rise Apt.	Dwelling Unit*	4	.40	.50
Mobile Home Park	Dwelling Unit*	5–6	.50	.60
Regional Shopping Center	1,000 sq.ft. of gross floor area	30–40	2.00	12.00
Community Shopping Center	1,000 sq.ft. of gross floor area	50–60	3.00	10.00
Industrial Park or Large General Office Building	Employee	3–4	1.00	1.00
Medical Clinic	Doctor	40–50	—	—
Motel	Occupied Unit	10	—	—
Golf Course	Hole	5–6	—	—
Hospital	Bed	10–12	—	—
High School	Student	1.40	—	—
Elementary School	Student	0.70	—	—

NOTE: In AM peak hours, 85% of all residential trips are expected to be out and 15% in. In the PM, 75% are expected to be in and 25% out. Office and industrial uses in the AM are expected to be 90% in and 10% out and just the opposite in the PM peak hour. Retail commercial is expected to be 55% in during the AM peak and 45% out, and during the PM peak, 70% out, 30% in.

*The chart is illustrative and the actual trip generation will vary with individual dwelling unit size.

197

| | **TRIPLE WIDE UNITS** | One mobile home living space created by joining three separate units together side to side. |

TRIPLE WIDE UNITS One mobile home living space created by joining three separate units together side to side.

TRIPLEX *See* DWELLING, TRIPLEX.

TRUCK CAMPER A structure designed to fit into the bed of a pick-up truck and used for temporary shelter and sleeping.

TRUCK STOP Any building, premises or land in which or upon which a business, service or industry involving the maintenance, servicing, storage or repair of commercial vehicles is conducted or rendered including the dispensing of motor fuel or other petroleum products directly into motor vehicles, the sale of accessories or equipment for trucks and similar commercial vehicles. A truck stop also may include overnight accommodations and restaurant facilities solely for the use of truck crews.

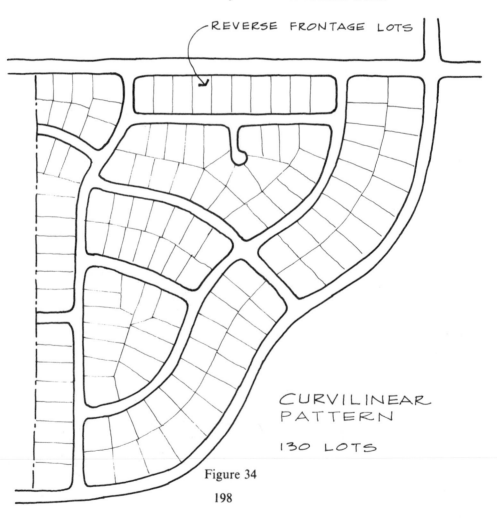

REVERSE FRONTAGE LOTS

CURVILINEAR PATTERN

130 LOTS

Figure 34

▦	**TRUCKING TERMINAL**	An area and building where cargo is stored and where trucks load and unload cargo on a regular basis.

TURBIDITY — A thick, hazy condition of air or water due to the presence of suspended particulates or other pollutants.

TUTORING — The provision of instruction to not more than two students at any given time.

Comment: Tutoring is usually considered a home occupation.

TWO-FAMILY DWELLING OR DUPLEX — *See* DWELLING, TWO-FAMILY.

U

UNDEVELOPED LAND — Land in its natural state before development.

UNIMPROVED LAND — Land in its natural state before development.

UNIVERSITY — *See* COLLEGE.

Comment: While there are technical differences between colleges and universities, for zoning purposes the difference is not important and no distinction need be made in the ordinance between the two uses.

UNIQUE NATURAL FEATURE — That part of the natural environment which is rare or not duplicated in the community or region.

UPLAND — Land elevated above surrounding lands.

UPZONE — To reduce the intensity of use by decreasing density or lowering the floor area ratio or otherwise increasing bulk requirements.

URBAN HOMESTEADING — A program for selling vacant, usually substandard urban housing to people who will rehabilitate and occupy such housing.

199

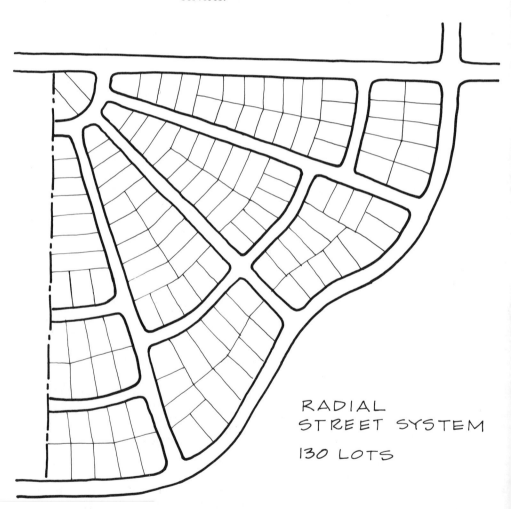

| | URBAN RENEWAL | A program for the physical improvement of primarily urban areas through comprehensive planning and governmental assistance to effect rehabilitation and redevelopment. |

| | URBAN RUNOFF | Storm water from city streets, gutters and paved surfaces. |

Comment: Urban runoff usually contains a great deal of litter and organic and bacterial wastes. *See* RUNOFF.

| | URBAN SERVICE BOUNDARY | A defined region, not always coincidental with a municipality's corporate boundary, that defines the geographical limit of government supplied public facilities and services. |

RADIAL
STREET SYSTEM
130 LOTS

Figure 35

USE	The purpose or activity for which land or buildings are designed, arranged, or intended, or for which land or buildings are occupied or maintained.	
USE, ACCESSORY	*See* ACCESSORY USE.	
USE, CONDITIONAL	*See* CONDITIONAL USE.	
USE, EXISTING	*See* EXISTING USE.	
USE, INSTITUTIONAL	*See* INSTITUTIONAL USE.	
USE, PERMITTED	*See* PERMITTED USE.	
USE, PRINCIPAL	*See* PRINCIPAL USE.	
USE, RELIGIOUS	*See* RELIGIOUS USE.	
USE, TEMPORARY	*See* TEMPORARY USE.	
USE, TRANSITIONAL	*See* TRANSITIONAL USE.	
USE VARIANCE	*See* VARIANCE, USE.	

UTILITY, PRIVATE OR PUBLIC

(1) Any agency which, under public franchise or ownership, or under certificate of convenience and necessity, provides the public with electricity, gas, heat, steam, communication, rail transportation, water, sewage collection, or other similar service; (2) A closely regulated private enterprise with an exclusive franchise for providing a public service.

UTILITY SERVICES

Establishments engaged in the generation, transmission and/or distribution of electricity, gas or steam, including water and irrigation systems and sanitary systems used for the collection and disposal of garbage, sewage and other wastes by means of destroying or processing materials.

V

VACANCY

Any unoccupied land, structure or part thereof which is available and suitable for occupancy.

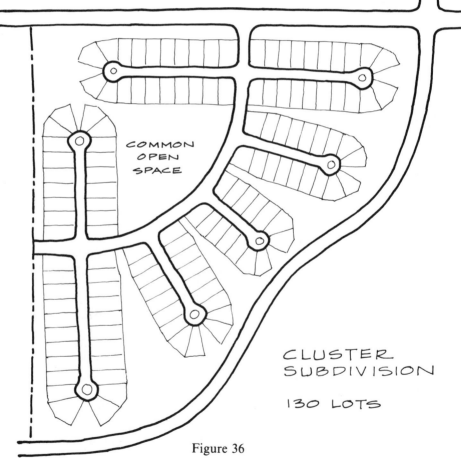

VACANCY RATE

The number of uninhabited dwelling units that are available and suitable for occupancy expressed as a ratio to the total number of housing units.

Comment: Vacancy rate may also apply to non-residential use and is usually expressed as a ratio of unoccupied floor area to total floor area.

VACANT LAND

See UNDEVELOPED LAND; UNIMPROVED LAND.

VACATION HOME

A second home, owned or rented, usually used seasonally, and located in an area with nearby recreational opportunities or amenities.

VALLEY

(1) A stretch of lowland lying between mountains or hills; (2) The land area drained or watered by a major river system.

COMMON
OPEN
SPACE

CLUSTER
SUBDIVISION

130 LOTS

Figure 36

202

VAN		(1) A closed vehicle with a capacity of approximately eight to twelve passengers; (2) A self-propelled recreation vehicle containing sleeping facilities but not bathroom or cooking facilities; (3) A large truck for carrying furniture or freight.

VANPOOLING

A share-the-expense method of commutation for approximately ten people who work in the same place and have the same work hours.

Comment: Vanpools differ from carpools in that the employer or sponsoring organization provides the vans that are used in the program.

VAPOR

The gaseous phase of substances that normally are either liquids or solids at atmospheric temperature and pressure; for example, steam and phenolic compounds.

VAPOR PLUME

Stack effluent consisting of condensed flue gas or flue gas made visible by condensed water droplets or mist.

VAPORIZATION

The change of a substance from the liquid to the gaseous state.

Comment: Vaporization is one of three basic contributing factors to air pollution, the others are attrition and combustion.

VARIANCE

Permission to depart from the literal requirements of a zoning ordinance.

VARIANCE, BULK

A departure from any provision of a zoning ordinance except use. *See* VARIANCE, HARDSHIP.

VARIANCE, HARDSHIP

A departure from the provisions of a zoning ordinance relating to setbacks, side yards, frontage requirements, and lot size, but not involving the actual use or structure.

Comment: The hardship variance is granted because strict enforcement of the zoning ordinance as it applies to a specific lot would work an undue hardship and present practical difficulties. It is usually granted to decrease the dimension requirements, and the applicant generally must demonstrate the hardship is peculiar to his property and not to other properties in the zone. The zoning board of adjustment or board of standards and appeals also must find that the variance can be granted without any adverse impact on the public good (the negative criteria).

203

VARIANCE, LOT

A departure from the yard, area, coverage, setback, size or other requirements of the applicable zoning district.

VARIANCE, USE

A variance granted for a use or structure that is not permitted in the zone.

Comment: Most states require that before a use variance can be granted, it must meet stringent requirements. In New Jersey the applicant must prove that the grant will not impair substantially the intent and purpose of the zone plan and ordinance and will be without substantial detriment to the public good. In addition, special reasons also must be present.

VEGETATIVE PROTECTION

Stabilization of erosive or sediment producing areas by covering the soil with permanent or short-term seeding, mulching, or sodding.

VEHICLE, MOTOR

A self-propelled device used for transportation of people or goods over land surfaces and licensed as a motor vehicle.

VEHICLE, RECREATIONAL

See RECREATIONAL VEHICLE.

VEHICULAR SALES AREA

An open area, other than a right-of-way or public parking area, used for display, sale or rental of new or used vehicles in operable condition and where no repair work is done.

 **VEST POCKET PARK**

A small land area, usually in a built up neighborhood, developed for active or passive recreation.

VOCATIONAL SCHOOL

A secondary or higher education facility primarily teaching usable skills that prepare students for jobs in a trade and meeting the state requirements as a vocational facility.

 VOLATILE

Evaporating readily at a relatively low temperature.

W

WADING POOL

An above-ground or inground structure containing less than eighteen inches of water.

204

	WALKUP	An apartment building of more than two stories that is not equipped with an elevator.
	WALKUP ESTABLISHMENT	An establishment that by design of its physical facilities, service, or packaging encourages or permits pedestrians to receive a service or obtain a product without entering the establishment.
	WALL	(1) The vertical exterior surface of a building; (2) Vertical interior surfaces which divide a building's space into rooms.
	WAREHOUSE	A building used primarily for the storage of goods and materials. *See* MINI-WAREHOUSE.
	WAREHOUSING	Terminal facilities for handling freight with or without maintenance facilities.
	WAREHOUSING, PRIVATE	Terminal facilities operated for a specific commercial establishment or group of establishments in a particular industrial or economic field.
	WAREHOUSING, PUBLIC	Terminal facilities available to the general public, at a fee, for the storage of farm products, furniture and other household goods, or commercial or private goods of any nature.
	WASTE	(1) Bulky Waste—Items the large size of which precludes or complicates their handling by normal collection, processing or disposal methods; (2) Construction and Demolition Waste—Building materials and rubble resulting from construction, remodeling, repair and demolition operations; (3) Hazardous Waste—Wastes that require special handling to avoid illness or injury to persons or damage to property; (4) Special Waste—Those wastes that require extraordinary management; (5) Wood Pulp Waste—Wood or paper fiber residue resulting from a manufacturing process; (6) Yard Waste—Plant clippings, prunings and other discarded material from yards and gardens.
	WASTELAND	Land that is barren and uncultivated.
	WASTEWATER	Water carrying wastes from homes, businesses and industries that is a mixture of water and dissolved or suspended solids, or excess irrigation water that is runoff to adjacent land.

205

◪ WATER BODIES

Any natural or artificial collection of water, whether permanent or temporary.

◪ WATER-CARRYING CAPACITY

The ability of a pipe, channel or floodway to transport flow as determined by its shape, cross-sectional area, bed slope, and coefficient of hydraulic friction.

▤▸▮◪ WATER COURSE

Any natural or artificial stream, river, creek, ditch, channel, canal, conduit, culvert, drain, waterway, gully, ravine or wash in which water flows in a definite direction or course, either continuously or intermittently, and has a definite channel, bed and banks, and includes any area adjacent thereto subject to inundation by reason of overflow or flood water.

▸▮◪ WATER POLLUTION

The addition of pollutants to water in concentrations or in sufficient quantities to result in measurable degradation of water quality.

◪ WATER QUALITY CRITERIA

The levels of pollutants that affect the suitablility of water for a given use.

Comment: Generally, water use classification includes public water supply, recreation, propagation of fish and other aquatic life, agricultural use and industrial use.

◪ WATER QUALITY STANDARD

A plan for water quality management containing four major elements: the use (recreation, drinking water, fish and wildlife propagation, industrial or agricultural) to be made of water; criteria to protect the water to keep it suitable for use; implementation plans (for needed industrial-municipal waste treatment improvements) and enforcement plans; and an antidegradation statement to protect existing high quality waters.

▤ ▮ WATER RIGHTS

A property owner's right to use surface or underground water from adjacent lands.

Comment: The western and eastern United States have different water rights laws. Riparian rights are applicable mainly to eastern areas. Western law generally provides that the first to claim the water has the use of it.

◪ WATER SUPPLY SYSTEM

The system for the collection, treatment, storage and distribution of potable water from the source of supply to the consumer.

WATER TABLE   The upper surface of groundwater, or that level below which the soil is seasonally saturated with water.

 WATER TRANSPORATION   Establishments engaged in freight and passenger transportation in the open seas or inland waters and the furnishing of incidental services such as lightering, towing and canal operation.

Comment: This major group includes excursion boats, sightseeing boats and water taxis, as well as cargo and hauling operations.

 **WATERFRONT PROPERTY**   A property that has frontage on a water body.

 WATERSHED   The area drained by a given stream or river. *See* RIVER BASIN.

 WETLANDS   Swamps or marshes, especially as areas preserved for wildlife.

WHOLESALE TRADE   Establishments or places of business primarily engaged in selling merchandise to retailers; to industrial, commercial, institutional, or professional business users, or to other wholesalers; or acting as agents or brokers and buying merchandise for, or selling merchandise to, such individuals or companies.

Comment: Lumber, plywood and millwork yards such as building materials establishments are generally classified as wholesale unless the primary operation is directly to the general public as opposed to builders. In such case, they are classified as retail operations.

Y

 YARD   An open space that lies between the principal or accessory building or buildings and the nearest lot line. Such yard is unoccupied and unobstructed from the ground upward except as may be specifically provided in the zoning ordinance. *See* BUILDABLE AREA; LOT LINE; YARD DEPTH; YARD LINE. *See Figure 20.*

YARD DEPTH   The shortest distance between a lot line and a yard line.

 YARD, FRONT   A space extending the full width of the lot between any building and the front lot line, and measured perpendicular to the building at the closest point to the front lot line. Such front yard is unoccupied and unobstructed from the ground upward except as may be permitted elsewhere in the ordinance. *See Figure 20.*

Comment: The definition specifies that the line of measurement is perpendicular to the building and extends to the lot line. If the line of measurement was perpendicular to the lot line, there would be problems with pie-shaped and irregular lots. The ordinance would normally specify that the front yard could contain fences, walls, driveways and whatever else may be customary in a particular zone.

 YARD LINE   A line drawn parallel to a lot line at a distance therefrom equal to the depth of the required yard. *See Figure 20.*

 YARD, REAR   A space extending across the full width of the lot between the principal building and the rear lot line, and measured perpendicular to the building to the closest point of the rear lot line. Such rear yard is unoccupied and unobstructed from the ground upward except as may be permitted elsewhere in the ordinance. *See Figure 20.*

Comment: See comment under YARD, FRONT.

 YARD, REQUIRED   The open space between a lot line and the buildable area within which no structure shall be located except as provided in the zoning ordinance. *See Figure 20.*

 YARD, SIDE   A space extending from the front yard to the rear yard between the principal building and the side lot line measured perpendicular from the side lot line to the closest point of the principal building., Such side yard is unoccupied and unobstructed from the ground upward except as may be permitted elsewhere in the ordinance. *See Figure 20.*

 YOUTH CAMP   Any parcel or parcels of land having the general characteristics of a camp as the term is generally understood, used wholly or part for recreational or educational purposes and accommodating five or more children under 18 years of age for a period of, or portions of, two days or more and including a site that is operated as a day camp or as a resident camp.

208

Z

ZERO LOT LINE   The location of a building on a lot in such a manner that one or more of the building's sides rest directly on a lot line.

ZONE   A specifically delineated area or district in a municipality within which regulations and requirements uniformly govern the use, placement, spacing and size of land and buildings. *See* FLOATING ZONE; TRANSITION ZONE.

ZONING   The dividing of a municipality into districts and the establishment of regulations governing the use, placement, spacing and size of land and buildings.

ZONING BOARD   *See* BOARD OF ADJUSTMENT.

ZONING DISTRICT   *See* ZONE.

ZONING ENVELOPE   The three-dimensional space within which a structure is permitted to be built on a lot and which is defined by maximum height regulations, yard setbacks, and sky exposure plane regulations.

ZONING MAP   The map or maps, which are a part of the zoning ordinance, and delineate the boundaries of zone districts.

ZONING OFFICER   The administrative officer designated to administer the zoning ordinance and issue zoning permits.

Comment: In many smaller communities, the building inspector is also the zoning officer.

ZONING PERMIT   A document signed by the zoning officer, as required in the zoning ordinance, as a condition precedent to the commencement of a use or the erection, construction, reconstruction, restoration, alteration, conversion, or installation of a structure or building, which acknowledges that such use, structure or building complies with the provisions of the municipal zoning or authorized variance therefrom.

Comment: Where a building permit is required, the building permit often includes a zoning permit.

Appendix/Index
Typical Ordinances In Which Definitions Are Usually Found

Most of the definitions contained in this book would be found in a land development ordinance. When separate ordinances are used, the following chart indicates in which ordinance a specific definition would normally appear. The chart also gives the page where the definition may be found.

— A —	Page Number	Zoning	Subdivision	Site Plan	Environmental	All
Abandonment	19	●				
Abatement	19				●	
Absorption	19				●	
Abut	19					●
Acceleration Lane	19		●	●		
Access	20					●
Access Road	20	●	●	●		
Accessory Structure	20	●		●		
Accessory Use	20	●		●		
Acclimatization	20				●	
Accretion	20				●	
Acre	20					●
Acre-Foot	21				●	
Activated Carbon	21				●	

211

	Page Number	Zoning	Subdivision	Site Plan	Environmental	All
Activated Sludge Process	21				●	
Adaptation	21	●		●	●	
Adaptive Reuse	21	●		●	●	
Addition	21	●		●		
Adjacent Land	21					●
Adjoining Lot or Land	21					●
Administrative Office	21					●
Administrative Officer	21					●
Adult Book Store	22	●				
Advanced Waste Treatment	22			●	●	●
Adverse Possession	22	●				
Advertising Display	22	●		●		
Aeration	22				●	
Aerial Map	22					●
Aerobic	22				●	
Aerosol	22				●	
Aesthetic	22	●		●	●	
Aesthetic Zoning	22	●			●	
Afterburner	23				●	
Agrarian	23	●				
Agricultural Market	23	●				
Agricultural Pollution	23				●	
Agricultural Services	23	●				
Agriculture	23	●				
Air Park	24	●				
Air Pollution	24	●		●	●	
Air Pollution Episode	24				●	
Air Quality Control Region	24				●	
Air Quality Criteria	24	●		●	●	
Air Quality Standards	24	●		●	●	

	Page Number	Zoning	Subdivision	Site Plan	Environmental	All
Air Rights	24	●		●		
Air Transportation	25	●				
Airport	25	●				
Aisle	25	●	●	●		
Alley	25	●	●	●		
Alluvion	25				●	
Alteration	26	●		●		
Ambient Air	26	●		●	●	
Ambient Air Standard	26	●		●	●	
Amenity	26					●
Amortization	26					●
Amusement And Recreation Services	26	●				
Amusement Facility	27	●				
Amusement Park	27	●				
Anchor Store	27	●				
Anchor Tenant	27	●				
Anerobic	27				●	
Animal Hospital	27	●				
Animal Kennel	27	●				
Animated Sign	27	●		●		
Annexation	27	●	●	●		
Anti-Degradation Clause	28				●	
Apartment, Garden	28	●		●		
Apartment, High-Rise	28	●		●		
Apartment House	28	●		●		
Apartment, Mid-Rise	28	●		●		
Apartment Unit	28	●		●		
Apartment Unit, Efficiency	28	●		●		
Applicant	28					●
Application for Development	28					●

	Page Number	Zoning	Subdivision	Site Plan	Environmental	All
Appraisal	28	●				
Approved Plan	28					●
Approving Authority	28					●
Aquaculture Project	28				●	
Aquarium	29	●				
Aquatic Plants	29				●	
Aquifer	29				●	
Aquifer Recharge Area	29				●	
Arcade	29	●		●		
Archaeological Site	29	●		●	●	
Architectural Control	30	●		●	●	
Area Scale	30					●
Area Source	30				●	
Arterial Street	30	●	●	●		
Artesian Aquifer	30				●	
Artificial Recharge	30		●		●	
Arts Center	30	●				
A-Scale Sound Level	30	●		●	●	
Assemblage	30	●	●			
Assessed Valuation	31	●	●	●		
Assessment Ratio	31	●	●	●		
Assimilation	31				●	
Atmosphere	31				●	
Attached Dwelling Unit	31	●				
Attention Getting Device	31	●		●		
Attic	31	●				
Audiometer	31	●		●		
Automatic Car Wash	32	●				
Automobile	32	●				
Automobile Repair	32	●				

	Page Number	Zoning	Subdivision	Site Plan	Environmental	All
Automobile Sales	32	●				
Automobile Service Station	32	●				
Automobile Wash	32	●				
Automobile Wrecking Yard	32	●				
Automotive Repair Services And Garages	32	●				
Autotrophic	32				●	
Aviation Easement	32	●		●		
Avulsion	32				●	
Awning	33	●		●		

— B —

	Page Number	Zoning	Subdivision	Site Plan	Environmental	All
Back-To-Back Lots	33	●	●	●		
Backfill	33			●	●	
Background Level	33				●	
Background Radiation	33				●	
Bacteria	33				●	
Baffle	33				●	
Baling	33	●				
Ballistic Separator	33				●	
Bar	33	●				
Bar Screen	34				●	
Barrier	34			●		
Barrier Island	34				●	
Base Flood Elevation	34					●
Base Map	34					●
Basement	34	●		●		
Basin	35					●
Beach	35					●
Bedrock	35		●	●	●	

	Page Number	Zoning	Subdivision	Site Plan	Environmental	All
Bedroom	35	●				
Beltway	35		●	●		
Berm	35					●
Bikeway	35		●	●		
Billboard	36	●		●		
Biochemical Biological Oxygen Demand	36				●	
Biodegradable	36				●	
Biological Control	36				●	
Biological Oxidation	36				●	
Biomonitoring	36				●	
Biosphere	36				●	
Biostabilizer	36				●	
Biota	36				●	
Blending	36				●	
Blighted Area	37	●				
Block	37					●
Block Statistics	37					●
Bloom	37				●	
Board of Adjustment	37	●	●	●		
Boarder	38	●				
Boarding Home For Sheltered Care	38	●				
Boarding House	38	●				
Boarding Stable	39	●				
Boardwalk	39			●		
Boatel	39	●				
Bog	39				●	
Bonus Zoning	39	●				
Borough	39					●
Brackish Water	39				●	
Breeding Farm	39	●				

	Page Number	Zoning	Subdivision	Site Plan	Environmental	All
Bridge	39					●
British Thermal Unit (BTU)	40				●	
Broadcast Application	40				●	
Brook	40					●
Buffer Strip	40					●
Buffer Zone	40					●
Buildable Area	40					●
Building	40					●
Building, Accessory	40					●
Building Coverage	40					●
Building Height	41	●	●	●		
Building Inspector	41					●
Building Line	41					●
Building Permit	41					●
Building, Principal	41					●
Built-Up Area	41					●
Bulk Envelope	41	●			●	
Bulkhead	41					●
Bulkhead Line	42					●
Bulk Plane	41	●			●	
Bulk Regulations	41	●			●	
Bulk Storage	42	●				
Bulletin Board Sign	42	●			●	
Bumpers	42	●			●	
Bus Shelter	42	●				
Bus Terminal or Station	42	●				
Bus Turnout	42	●		●	●	
Business Services	42	●				
Business Sign	43	●			●	
Busway	43	●				

	Page Number	Zoning	Subdivision	Site Plan	Environmental	All
Certificate of Compliance	47					•
Certificate of Need	47					•
Certificate of Occupancy (CO)	47					•
Certification	47					•
Cession Deed	47	•	•	•		
Cesspool	47		•	•	•	
CFS	47		•	•	•	
Chain	48					•
Chain Store	48	•				
Change of Use	48	•		•		
Channel	48		•	•	•	
Channelization	48		•	•	•	
Charitable Use	49	•				
Chattel	49	•	•	•		
Chemical Oxygen Demand (COD)	49				•	
Child Care Center	49	•				
Chimney	49	•		•		
Chlorinated Hydrocarbons	49				•	
Chlorination	49				•	
Chlorinator	50				•	
Chlorosis	50				•	
Christmas Tree Farm	50	•				
Church	50	•				
Circulation	50					•
Cistern	50				•	
Citizen Participation	51					•
City Planning	51					•
Civic Center	51	•				
Clarification	51				•	
Clarifier	51				•	

	Page Number	Zoning	Subdivision	Site Plan	Environmental	All
Clean Air Act	51				●	
Clinic	51	●				
Cloverleaf	51			●	●	
Club	51	●				
Clubhouse	52	●				
Cluster	52					●
Cluster Subdivision	52					●
Cohabitation	52	●				
Coliform Index	52				●	
Coliform Organism	52				●	
College	53	●				
Colliery	53	●				
Colosseum	53	●				
Combined sewers	53			●	●	●
Combustion	53				●	
Commercial Condominium	53	●				
Commercial Garage	53	●				
Commercial Greenhouse	53	●				
Commercial Use	53	●				
Commercial Vehicle	53	●				
Comminution	53				●	
Comminutor	53				●	
Common Elements	54					●
Common Open Space	54					●
Common Ownership	54					●
Common Passageway	54					●
Communication Use	54	●				
Community Association	54					●
Community Center	54	●				
Community Facility	54	●				

	Page Number	Zoning	Subdivision	Site Plan	Environmental	All
Community Impact Study	54		●	●	●	
Compaction	54				●	
Complete Application	54					●
Compost	55				●	
Composting	55				●	
Comprehensive Plan	55					●
Concept Plan	55					●
Condemnation	55					●
Conditional Use	55	●		●	●	
Conditional Use Permit	56	●		●	●	
Condominium	56					●
Condominium Association	56					●
Condominium, Commercial	56	●				
Condominium Hotel	56	●				
Condominium, Industrial	56	●				
Condominium, Office	57	●				
Conference Center	57	●				
Congregate Housing	57	●				
Conservation District	57					●
Conservation Easement	57					●
Consideration	57					●
Consolidation	57					●
Construction Official	57					●
Construction Permit	57					●
Contiguous	58					●
Continuing Easement	58					●
Convention Facility	58	●				
Conventional Energy System	58	●			●	
Conversion	58					●
Cooling Tower	58				●	

	Page Number	Zoning	Subdivision	Site Plan	Environmental	All
Corner Lot	58					●
Cost-Benefit Analysis	58					●
Cottage	59	●	●			
Cottage Industry	59	●				
Council of Governments	59					●
Country Club	59	●				
County Master Plan	59					●
Court	59	●		●		
Court, Inner	60	●		●		
Court, Outer	60	●		●		
Cove	60				●	
Covenant	60					●
Cover Material	60					●
Coverage	60					●
Crawl Space	60	●				
Creek	61					●
Critical Area	61					●
Crop	61	●				
Cubic Content	61					●
Cul-De-Sac	61	●	●	●		
Cultural Eutrophication	61				●	
Cultural Facilities	62	●				
Culvert	62		●	●	●	
Curb	62		●	●		
Curb Cut	62		●	●		
Curb Level	62		●	●		
Curb Return	62		●	●		
Current	62				●	
Current Planning Capacity	62					●

	Page Number	Zoning	Subdivision	Site Plan	Environmental	All
Curvilinear Street System	62		•	•		
Cut	62		•	•	•	

— D —

	Page Number	Zoning	Subdivision	Site Plan	Environmental	All
Datum	63					•
Datum Plane	63					•
Day Care Center/Day Nursery	63	•				
DDT	63				•	
Dead End Street	63	•	•	•		
Deceleration Lane	63		•	•		
Decibel	63	•		•	•	
Deciduous	63					•
Deck Line	64	•		•		
Decomposition	64				•	
Dedication	64					•
Deed	64					•
Deed Restriction	64					•
Demography	64					•
Demolition (Permit)	64					•
Density	64					•
Density Modification Subdivision	65	•	•			
Desalinization	65				•	
Desiccant	65				•	
Detention Basin (Pond)	65					•
Detergent	65				•	
Deterioration	65					•
Developer	65					•

223

	Page Number	Zoning	Subdivision	Site Plan	Environmental	All
Development	65					•
Development Analysis Study	65					•
Development, Conventional	65					•
Development, Major	66					•
Development, Minor	66					•
Development, Planned	66					•
Development Regulation	66					•
Development Timing	66					•
Diatomaceous Earth (Diatomite)	66				•	
Diffused Air	66				•	
Digester	66				•	
Digestion	67				•	
Dilapidation	67					•
Dilution Ratio	67				•	
Discount Center	67	•				
Disposal Area	67		•	•	•	
Disposal Bed	67		•	•	•	
Disposal Field	67		•	•	•	
Disposal Trench	67		•	•	•	
Dissolved Oxygen (DO)	68				•	
Dissolved Solids	68				•	
Distance of Sign Projection	68	•		•		
Distribution Box	68		•	•	•	
Distribution Lines	68		•	•	•	
District	68					•
Diversion Channel	68					•
Domicile	68	•				
Donation	68					•
Dormer	68	•				
Dormitory	68	•				

	Page Number	Zoning ⊞	Subdivision ⚑	Site Plan ⌐	Environmental ▲	All
Dose	69				•	
Dosimeter	69				•	
Dosing Tanks	69				•	
Double Wide Unit	69	•	•			
Down Zone	69	•				
Drainage	69					•
Drainage Area	69					•
Drainage District	69					•
Drainage System	69					•
Drainageway	69					•
Dredge And Fill	70					•
Dredging	70					•
Drive-In Restaurant	70	•				
Drive-In Theater	70	•				
Drive-In Use	70	•				
Driveway	70	•	•	•		
Drug Store	70	•				
Drywell	71		•	•	•	
Dump	71	•			•	
Duplex	71	•				
Dwelling	71					•
Dwelling, Attached	71	•		•		
Dwelling, Detached	71	•	•			
Dwelling, Garden Apartment	72	•		•		
Dwelling, High-Rise	72	•		•		
Dwelling, Mid-Rise	72	•		•		
Dwelling, Multifamily	72	•		•		
Dwelling, Patio House	73	•		•		
Dwelling, Quadruplex	73	•		•		
Dwelling, Semidetached	73	•		•		

226

	Page Number	Zoning	Subdivision	Site Plan	Environmental	All
			▨	▶	◣	▲
Effluent	79				●	
Egress	79					●
Eleemosynary or Philanthropic Institution	79	●				
Elevation	79					●
Embankment	79		●	●	●	
Eminent Domain	79					●
Emission	79				●	
Emission Factor	80				●	
Emission Inventory	80				●	
Emission Standard	80				●	
Enabling Act	80					●
Encroachment	80					●
Enlargement	80					●
Enrichment	80				●	
Environment	80				●	
Environmental Impact Statement (EIS)	80					●
Environmentally Sensitive Area	81					●
Erosion	81					●
Essential Services	81	●				
Establishment	81	●				
Estuaries	81	●		●	●	
Eutrophic Lakes	81				●	
Eutrophication	82				●	
Evaluation	82					●
Evaporation Ponds	82				●	
Excavation	82					●
Exclusionary Zoning	82	●				
Exclusive Use District	82	●				
Existing Grade or Elevation	82					●
Existing Use	83	●				

	Page Number	Zoning	Subdivision	Site Plan	Environmental	All
Exit Ramp, Entrance Ramp	83			●	●	
Extended Care Facility	83	●				
Extension	83					●
Exterior Wall	83	●		●		

— F —

	Page Number	Zoning	Subdivision	Site Plan	Environmental	All
Fabrication And Assembly	83	●				
Facade	83	●		●		
Factory	84	●				
Factory-Built House	84	●				
Fair Market Value	84	●		●		
Fair Share Housing Plans	84	●				
Fallow Land	84				●	
Family	84	●				
Farm or Farmland	85	●			●	
Farm Stand	85	●				
Farm Structure	85	●				
Fast-Food Restaurant	85	●				
Fault Area	86				●	
Feasibility Study	86					●
Fee Simple Absolute	86		●			
Feedlot	86	●				
Fen	86				●	
Fence	86					●
Fill	86					●
Filling	86					●
Filling Station	86	●				
Filtration	87				●	

	Page Number	Zoning	Subdivision	Site Plan	Environmental	All
Final Approval	87					●
Final Plan	87					●
Finance, Insurance And Real Estate	87	●				
Finger Fill Canals	87					●
Finish Elevation	87					●
Finished Product	87	●				
Fish Farm	87	●				
Fishing, Hunting, Trapping	87	●				
Flag Lot	88	●	●			
Flea Market	88	●				
Floating Zone	88	●				
Flocculation	89				●	
Flood	89					●
Flood, Base Flood Elevation	89					●
Flood Damage Potential	89					●
Flood Fringe Area	89					●
Flood Hazard Area	89					●
Flood Hazard Design Elevation	89					●
Flood Insurance Rate Map	89		●	●	●	
Flood Of Record	89					●
Flood, Regulatory Base	89					●
Flood, Regulatory Base Flood Discharge	90					●
Flood Plain	90					●
Floodproofing	90		●	●	●	
Floodway	90					●
Floodway, Regulatory	90					●
Floor Area, Gross	91	●		●		
Floor Area, Net	91	●		●		
Floor Area Ratio	91	●		●		
Floriculture	91	●				

	Page Number	Zoning	Subdivision	Site Plan	Environmental	All
Garage, Private Customer And Empl.	94	●			●	
Garage, Private Residential	95	●		●		
Garage, Public	95	●			●	
Garage, Repair	95	●				
Garbage	95					●
Garden Apartment	95	●			●	
Gasoline Station	95	●				
General Public	95					●
Glare	95				●	
Golf Course	95	●				
Government Agency	95					●
Grade	96					●
Grade, Finished	96					●
Grade, Natural	96					●
Grading	96			●	●	●
Grain Loading	96	●				
Grant	96					●
Graphic Scale	96					●
Gravel Pit	96	●				
Grease Trap	97					●
Green Area	97					●
Greenbelt	97					●
Greenhouse	97	●				
Grid System	97			●		
Gross Floor Area	97	●			●	
Gross Habitable Floor Area	97	●			●	
Gross Leasable Area	97	●			●	
Ground Cover	97	●			●	●
Ground Coverage	97	●			●	
Ground Floor	97	●		●	●	

	Page Number	Zoning	Subdivision	Site Plan	Environmental	All
Highest And Best Use	102	●				
Highway	102		●	●		
Historic Area	102	●			●	
Historic Building	102	●		●	●	
Historic Building Styles	102	●		●	●	
Historic District	102	●		●	●	
Historic Preservation	102	●		●	●	
Historic Site	104	●		●	●	
Hi-Volume (HI-VOL) Sampler	104				●	
Home Occupation	104	●	●			
Home Professional Office	104	●	●			
Homeowners Association	105	●	●			
Horticulture	105	●				
Hospital	105	●				
Hotel	105	●				
House Trailer	105	●				
Household	105	●				
Housing Assistance Plan (HAP)	106	●				
Housing For The Elderly	106	●				
Housing Region	106	●				
Housing Unit	107	●				
Humus	107				●	
Hydrology	107				●	

— I —

	Page Number	Zoning	Subdivision	Site Plan	Environmental	All
Impact Analysis	107				●	
Impedance	107				●	
Impermeable	107	●		●	●	
Impervious Surface	107	●		●	●	

233

	Page Number	Zoning	Subdivision	Site Plan	Environmental	All
Implementation	107					•
Impoundment	107		•	•	•	
Improved Lot	108					•
Improvement	108					•
Incentive Zoning	108	•				
Incineration	108				•	
Incinerator	108	•			•	
Inclusion Zoning	108	•				
Indirect Source	109				•	
Individual Sewage Disposal System	109	•		•	•	
Indoor Tennis Facility	109	•				
Industrial Park	109	•		•		
Industrial Property	109	•				
Industrial Separator	109				•	
Industrial Waste	109				•	
Industry	109	•				
Industry, Light	109	•				
In-Fill Development	110	•		•		
Infiltration	110				•	
Infrastructure	110					•
Ingress	110					•
Inn	110	•				
Institutional Use	110	•				
Interceptor Sewer	110					•
Interchange	110			•	•	
Interested Party	110					•
Interior Lot	111	•		•		
Intermediate Care Facility	111	•				
Intersection	111	•		•	•	
Interstate Highway System	111			•	•	

234

	Page Number	Zoning	Subdivision	Site Plan	Environmental	All
Interstate Waters	111				•	
Intertidal Area	111				•	
Inverse Condemnation	111					•
Inversion	111				•	
Island	112					•
Isolated Lot	112	•	•			

— J —

	Page Number	Zoning	Subdivision	Site Plan	Environmental	All
Joint Ownership	112	•	•	•		
Journey To Work	113	•				
Junction	113		•	•		
Junk	113	•			•	
Junkyard	113	•				
Just Compensation	113					•

— K —

	Page Number	Zoning	Subdivision	Site Plan	Environmental	All
Kennel	113	•				
Kiosk	113	•	•	•		

— L —

	Page Number	Zoning	Subdivision	Site Plan	Environmental	All
Labor Force	114	•				
Lagoon	114	•		•	•	
Lake	114				•	
Land	114					•
Land Bank	114			•	•	
Land Disturbance	114				•	
Land Reclamation	114				•	

	Page Number	Zoning	Subdivision	Site Plan	Environmental	All
Land Surveyor	114					●
Land Use	114					●
Land Use Intensity (LUI) Standards	114	●				
Land Use Plan	115					●
Landfill	115		●	●	●	
Landmark	115	●			●	
Landscape	115				●	
Large Lot Zoning	115	●				
Lateral Sewer	115			●	●	
Laundromat	115	●				
Leachate	115				●	
Leaching	116				●	
Lease	116					●
Least Cost Housing	116	●				
Less-Than-Fee Acquisition	116					●
Life Cycle	116	●				
Lift	116				●	
Light Industry	116	●				
Light Plane	117	●		●		
Limnology	117				●	
Lines	117					●
Littoral	117				●	
Littoral Drift	117				●	
Littoral Land	118				●	
Loading Space	118	●		●		
Local Authority	118					●
Local Housing Authority	118	●				
Local Improvement	118					●
Lodge	118	●				
Lodger	118	●				

	Page Number	Zoning	Subdivision	Site Plan	Environmental	All
Lodging House	118	●				
Long-Term Care Facility	118	●				
Lot	119	●	●	●		
Lot Area	119	●	●	●		
Lot Averaging	119					●
Lot, Corner	119	●	●			
Lot Coverage	119	●	●	●		
Lot Depth	119	●	●	●		
Lot, Double Frontage	119	●	●	●		
Lot, Flag	120	●	●			
Lot Frontage	120	●	●	●		
Lot, Interior	120	●	●	●		
Lot, Isolated	120	●	●	●		
Lot Line	120	●	●	●		
Lot Line, Front	120	●	●	●		
Lot Line, Rear	120	●	●	●		
Lot Line, Side	121	●	●	●		
Lot, Minimum Area Of	121	●	●	●		
Lot of Record	121	●	●	●		
Lot, Reverse Frontage	121	●	●			
Lot, Through	121	●	●	●		
Lot, Transition	121	●	●	●		
Lot Width	121	●	●	●		
Low-Income Housing	121	●				
— M —						
Made Land	122	●			●	
Magnet Store	122	●				
Maintenance Guarantee	122					●

	Page Number	Zoning	Subdivision	Site Plan	Environmental	All
Mall	122	•				
Manufacturing	122	•				
Map, Contour	123					•
Map, Official	123					•
Marina	123	•				
Marketability Study	123	•		•		
Marquee	123	•				
Marshlands	123				•	
Masking	123				•	
Mass Transit	123	•				
Master Deed	123	•	•	•		
Master Plan	124					•
Mean	124					•
Mean High Water Line	124				•	
Mechanical Turbulence	124				•	
Median	124					•
Median Island	124			•	•	
Medical Building	124	•				
Megalopolis	124					•
Membership Organization	125	•				
Mesotrophic Lakes	125				•	
Meter	125					•
Metes And Bounds	125					•
Metric System	125					•
Metropolis	125					•
Metropolitan Area	125					•
Mezzanine	125	•				
MGD	125				•	
Mid-Rise	125	•		•		
Migration	125					•

	Page Number	Zoning	Subdivision	Site Plan	Environmental	All
Mile	125					•
Mill	126	•				
Mine	126	•			•	
Mineral Rights	126	•			•	
Mini-Mall	126	•				
Minimum Habitable Floor Area	126	•		•		
Mining	126	•			•	
Mini-Warehouse	126	•				
Mist	127				•	
Mixed Liquor	127				•	
Mixed Use Development (MXD)	127	•		•		
Mixed Use Zoning	127	•				
Mobile Home	127	•				
Mobile Home Park	127	•		•		
Mobile Home Space	128	•	•			
Mobile Source	128				•	
Modal Split	128			•		
Mode	128					•
Moderate-Income Housing	128	•				
Moratorium	128					•
Morbidity Rate	128				•	
Morgue	128	•				
Mortality Rate	128				•	
Mortuary	129	•				
Motel	129	•				
Motion Picture Theater	129	•				
Motor Freight Terminal	129	•				
Mulch	129				•	
Mulching	129				•	
Multifamily Dwelling	129	•		•		

	Page Number	Zoning	Subdivision	Site Plan	Environmental	All
Multi-Phase Development	129	•			•	
Multi-Use Building	129	•				
Municipality	129					•

— N —

	Page Number	Zoning	Subdivision	Site Plan	Environmental	All
National Environment Policy Act	130				•	
National Flood Insurance Program	130					•
National Historic Preservation Act	130					•
National Register of Historic Places	130					•
National Wild and Scenic Rivers System	130					•
Natural Drainage Flow	130		•	•	•	
Natural Grade	130					•
Natural Ground Surface	130					•
Natural Monument	130					•
Natural Recharge	130		•	•	•	
Natural Resources Inventory (NRI)	131					•
Natural Selection	131				•	
Negative Easement	132					•
Neighborhood	132	•	•	•		
Neighboring Dwelling	132	•	•	•		
Net Area of Lot (Net Acreage)	132	•				
New Car Agency	132	•				
New Town or New Community	132	•				
Noise	132	•		•	•	
Noise Pollution	132	•		•	•	
Nonconforming Lot	133	•	•			
Nonconforming Sign	133	•		•		
Nonconforming Structure or Building	133	•		•		
Nonconforming Use	133	•				

	Page Number	Zoning	Subdivision	Site Plan	Environmental	All
Non-Point Runoff	133				●	
Nuisance	133		●		●	
Nuisance Element	133		●		●	
Nursery	133		●			
Nursery School	133		●			
Nursing Home	133		●			

— O —

	Page Number	Zoning	Subdivision	Site Plan	Environmental	All
Obstruction	134					●
Occupancy or Occupied	134					●
Occupancy Permit	134					●
Occupancy Rate	134		●	●	●	
Occupant	134		●	●	●	
Occupation	134		●			
Odd-Lot Development	134		●	●		
Odorous Matter	134				●	
Offer	135					●
Office	135		●			
Office Building	135		●		●	
Office Park	135		●		●	
Office-At-Home	135		●	●	●	
Official Map	135					●
Official Soil Map	135					●
Official Soils Interpretation	135					●
Off-Site	135					●
Off-Street Parking Space	136		●	●	●	
Off-Tract	136					●
Oligotrophic Lakes	136				●	
One Hundred Percent Location	136			●		

	Page Number	Zoning	Subdivision	Site Plan	Environmental	All
On Site	136					●
On-Street Parking Space	136	●	●	●		
On Tract	136					●
Opacity	136				●	
Open Burning	136				●	
Open Dump	136	●			●	
Open Meeting or Hearing	136					●
Open Space	137					●
Open Space, Common	137					●
Open Space, Green	137					●
Open Space, Private	137					●
Open Space, Public	137					●
Open Space Ratio	137	●		●	●	
Option	137					●
Ordinance	137					●
Organic	137				●	
Organism	137				●	
Origin And Destination Study	137	●		●		
Outbuilding	137	●				
Outdoor Storage	138	●				
Outfall	138				●	
Overfire Air	138				●	
Overflow Rights	138				●	
Overflowed Land	138				●	
Overhang	138	●				
Owner	138					●
Oxidation Pond	138				●	
Ozone	138				●	

	Page Number	Zoning	Subdivision	Site Plan	Environmental	All
— P —						
Package Plant	139					●
Packed Tower	139				●	
Pad	139				●	
Parapet	139		●		●	
Parcel	139					●
Park	139					●
Parking Access	139		●	●	●	
Parking Area	139		●	●	●	
Parking Area, Private	139		●	●	●	
Parking Area, Public	139		●		●	
Parking Bay	140		●	●	●	
Parking Lot	140		●		●	
Parking Space	140		●	●	●	
Parochial School	140		●			
Partial Taking	140					●
Particulate Loading	140				●	
Particulates	140				●	
Party Driveway	140		●	●	●	
Party Immediately Concerned	140					●
Party Wall	140		●	●	●	
Path	140				●	
Pathogenic	140				●	
Patio	140			●	●	●
Pavement	140					●
Peak Hour Traffic	141					●
Peat	141				●	

	Page Number	Zoning	Subdivision 🏁	Site Plan ⌐•	Environmental ◤	Environmental ⛰	All
Pedestrian	141						●
Pedestrian Scale	141						●
Pedestrian Traffic Count	141						●
Peninsula	141				●		
Penthouse	141	●					
People Mover	141			●			
Percolating Area	142		●		●		
Percolation	142		●		●		
Percolation Test	142		●		●		
Performance Guarantee	142						●
Performance Standards	142						●
Perimeter	142						●
Perimeter Landscaped Open Space	142			●			
Permafrost	142				●		
Permeability	142		●		●		
Permit	142						●
Permitted Use	142	●					
Permittee	142						●
Person	143						●
Personal Services	143	●					
Pervious Surface	143			●	●		
Pesticide	143				●		
Pesticide Tolerance	143				●		
pH	143				●		
Pharmacy	143	●					
Phenols	143				●		
Photochemical Smog	144				●		
Pierhead Line	144				●		
Pig	144				●		
Pile	144				●		

	Page Number	Zoning	Subdivision	Site Plan	Environmental	All
Pilot Plant	144		●			
Plankton	144				●	
Planned Commercial Development	144		●		●	
Planned Development	144		●		●	
Planned Industrial Development	145		●		●	
Planned Unit Development (PUD)	145		●		●	
Planned Unit Residential Devel. (PURD)	145		●		●	
Planning Board	145					●
Plat	145			●		
Plat, Final	145			●		
Plat, Preliminary	145			●		
Plat, Sketch	145			●		
Plaza	146		●		●	
Plot	146					●
Plume	146				●	
Point Source	146				●	
Pollutant	146				●	
Pollution	146				●	
Porch	146		●			
Porosity	146			●	●	
Potable Water	146					●
PPM	146				●	
Precipitate	146				●	
Precipitation	146				●	
Pre-Emptive Right	147					●
Preliminary Approval	147					●
Preliminary Floor Plans And Elevations	147			●	●	
Preliminary Plan	147					●
Premises	147		●			
Prescription	147		●			

	Page Number	Zoning	Subdivision	Site Plan	Environmental	All
		■		⌐	◣	
Preservation, Historic	147					●
Pretreatment	147				●	
Primary Treatment	147				●	
Principal Building	147	●				
Principal Use	148	●				
Private Club or Lodge	148	●				
Private School	148	●				
Probablilty	148				●	
Process Weight	148				●	
Processing	148	●				
Processing and Warehousing	148	●				
Professional Office	149	●				
Prohibited Use	149	●				
Project	149					●
Projection	149	●				
Property Line	149					●
Protective Covenant	149					●
Public Administration	149					●
Public Area	149					●
Public Development Proposal	149					●
Public Domain	150					●
Public Drainage Way	150					●
Public Garage	150	●		●		
Public Hearing	150					●
Public Housing	150	●				
Public Improvement	150					●
Public Notice	150					●
Public Sewer And Water System	151					●
Public Transit System	151					●
Public Utility	151					●

246

	Page Number	Zoning	Subdivision	Site Plan	Environmental	All
Public Utility Facilities	151					●
Pulverization	151				●	
Pumping Station	151		●	●	●	
Putrescible	151				●	

— Q —

	Page Number	Zoning	Subdivision	Site Plan	Environmental	All
Quadruplex	151	●		●		
Quarry	151	●			●	
Quarter Section	151		●			
Quasi-Public	152					●
Quench Tank	152				●	
Quorum	152					●

— R —

	Page Number	Zoning	Subdivision	Site Plan	Environmental	All
Rad	152				●	
Radial Street System	152		●			
Radiation	152				●	
Radiation Standards	152				●	
Rainfall, Excess	152				●	
Ramp	152			●		
Ranch	153	●				
Rasp	153				●	
Ratable Property	153					●
Ravine	153				●	
Raw Sewage	153				●	
Rear Yard	153	●	●	●		
Reasonable Use Doctrine	153					●
Receiving Waters	153		●	●	●	

	Page Number	Zoning	Subdivision	Site Plan	Environmental	All
Recharge	153				●	
Reclaimed Land	153				●	
Recreation, Active	153	●		●	●	
Recreation Facility	153	●				
Recreation Facility, Commercial	154	●			●	
Recreation Facility, Personal	154	●		●		
Recreation Facility, Private	154	●		●	●	
Recreation Facility, Public	154	●			●	
Recreation, Passive	154	●		●	●	
Recreational Development	154	●			●	
Recreational Vehicle	154	●				
Recreational Vehicle Park	154	●				
Rectilinear Street System	154			●		
Recycling	154				●	
Refuse	154			●	●	
Refuse Reclamation	154				●	
Region	155					●
Regional Shopping Center	155	●				
Regulatory Base Flood	155					●
Regulatory Base Flood Discharge	155					●
Regulatory Floodway	155					●
Rehabilitation	155	●				
Regilious Use	155	●				
Relocate	155	●		●		
Rent	155	●				
Repair Garage	155	●				
Research Laboratory	155	●				
Reservation	156					●
Reservoir	156					●
Residence	156	●				

249

	Page Number	Zoning	Subdivision	Site Plan	Environmental	All
		▨	⚑	◪	▲	
Riparian Grant	160				•	
Riparian Land	160				•	
Riparian Rights	160				•	
River	160					•
River Basin	161					•
Road	161					•
Rod	161					•
Roof	161	•				
Roof, Flat	161	•				
Roof, Gable	161	•				
Roof, Gambrel	161	•				
Roof, Hip	161	•				
Roof, Mansard	161	•				
Roof, Shed	161	•				
Roomer	161	•				
Rooming House	161	•				
Rooming Unit	161	•				
Row House	161	•		•		
Rubbish	162			•	•	
Run With The Land	162					•
Runoff	162		•	•	•	
Rural Area	162					•
– S –						
Sale	163					•
Saline Land	163				•	
Salinity	163				•	
Salt Water Intrusion	163				•	
Salvage	163	•			•	

	Page Number	Zoning	Subdivision	Site Plan	Environmental	All
Sampling	163				●	
Sand Pit	163	●				
Sanitary Land Fill	163	●			●	
Sanitary Landfilling	163				●	
Sanitary Sewage	163					●
Sanitary Sewers	163					●
Sanitation	164	●				
Sanitorium	164	●				
Scale	164					●
Scattered Site Housing	164	●				
Scenic Area	164					●
Scenic Easement	164					●
School	164	●				
School District	165					●
School, Elementary	165	●				
School, Parochial	165	●				
School, Private	165	●				
School, Secondary	165	●				
School, Vocational	165	●				
Scrap	165	●			●	
Screening	166			●	●	
Scrubber	166				●	
Sea Level	166					●
Sea Shore	166					●
Seasonal Dwelling Unit	166	●				
Seasonal Structure	166	●				
Seasonal Use	166	●				
Seawall	166				●	
Second Home Community	166	●				
Secondary Treatment	166				●	

251

	Page Number	Zoning	Subdivision	Site Plan	Environmental	All
Section of Land	167					•
Sediment	167					•
Sediment Basin	167					•
Sedimentation	167					•
Sedimentation Tanks	167					•
Seepage	167				•	
Seepage Pit	167				•	
Semidetached	167	•				
Semifinished Product	167	•				
Senior Citizen Housing	168	•				
Septic System	168			•	•	
Septic Tank	168			•	•	
Service Station	168	•				
Services	168	•				
Setback	169	•	•	•		
Setback Line	169	•	•	•		
Settleable Solids	169				•	
Settling Chamber	169				•	
Settling Tank	169				•	
Sewage	169					•
Sewer	170					•
Sewer System And Treatment	170					•
Sewerage	170					•
Sheltered Care Facility	170	•				
Shield	170				•	
Shopping Center	170	•				
Side Yard	171	•	•	•		
Sidewalk	171	•	•	•		
Sight Triangle	171	•	•	•		
Sign	172	•		•		

	Page Number	Zoning	Subdivision	Site Plan	Environmental	All
Sign, Wall	175	●		●		
Sign, Warning	175	●	●	●		
Sign, Window	175	●		●		
Silt	175		●	●	●	
Silviculture	175				●	
Single Ownership	176	●				
Single-Family Dwelling	176	●	●			
Sinking	176				●	
Site	176					●
Site Plan	176					●
Skateboard Park	176	●				
Sketch Plan	176		●	●		
Ski Area	176	●				
Ski Resort	176	●				
Skilled Nursing Home	177	●				
Skimming	177				●	
Sky Exposure Plane	177	●		●		
Slope	177					●
Sludge	177				●	
Slum	177					●
Smog	177				●	
Smoke	177				●	
Social Services	177	●				
Soil	177					●
Soil Conditioner	177					●
Soil Conservation District	178					●
Soil Engineer	178					●
Soil Erosion	179					●
Soil Erosion and Sediment Control Plan	179					●
Soil Map	179					●

254

	Page Number	Zoning	Subdivision	Site Plan	Environmental	All
Solar Access	179					●
Solar Energy System	179					●
Solar Skyspace	179					●
Solar Skyspace Easement	180					●
Solid Waste	180	●		●	●	
Solid Waste Disposal	180	●		●	●	
Solid Waste Management	180	●		●	●	
Sonic Boom	180				●	
Soot	181				●	
Sorority House	181	●				
Special Assessment	181					●
Special District	181					●
Special Exception Use	181	●				
Special Use Permit	181	●				
Specialty Food Store	181	●				
Specialty Shopping Center	181	●				
Specifications	181					●
Speed Bump	181		●	●		
Spoil	181				●	
Spot Zoning	182	●				
Square	182	●		●		
Squatter	182	●				
Stabilization	182				●	
Stable	182	●				
Stack	182				●	
Stadium	182	●				
Stall	182	●		●		
Standard Metro. Statistical Area (SMSA)	183					●
Standard Of Living	183					●
Stationary Source	184				●	

	Page Number	Zoning	Subdivision	Site Plan	Environmental	All
Steep Slope	184				•	
Storm Sewer	184		•	•	•	
Stormwater Detention	184		•	•	•	
Story	184	•				
Story, Half	184	•				
Stream	184					•
Street	184	•	•	•		
Street, Collector	185	•	•	•		
Street, Cul-De-Sac	185	•	•	•		
Street, Dead End	185	•	•	•		
Street, Dual	185	•	•	•		
Street, Expressway	185	•	•	•		
Street, Freeway	186	•	•	•		
Street Furniture	186	•	•	•		
Street Hardware	186	•	•	•		
Street Line	186	•	•	•		
Street, Local	186	•	•	•		
Street, Loop	186	•	•	•		
Street, Major Arterial	186	•	•	•		
Street, Minor Arterial	186	•	•	•		
Street, Service	186	•	•	•		
Strip Development	186	•		•		
Strip Mining	186	•			•	
Strip Zoning	186	•				
Structural Alteration	187	•				
Structure	187	•		•		
Stud Farm	187	•				
Studio	187	•				
Studio Apartment	187	•				
Subdivider	187		•			

256

	Page Number	Zoning	Subdivision	Site Plan	Environmental	All
Subdivision	187		•			
Subdivision, Cluster	187	•	•			
Subdivision, Consolidation	187	•	•			
Subdivision, Major	188		•			
Subdivision, Minor	188		•			
Submerged Land	188				•	
Subsidence	188				•	
Subsidized Housing	188	•				
Subsoil	188		•	•	•	
Substandard Structure/Dwelling	188	•				
Substantial Improvement	188					•
Sulfur Dioxide (SO$_2$)	188				•	
Sump	188				•	
Supermarket	189	•				
Surface Water	189					•
Surfactant	189				•	
Surgical Center	189	•				
Surveillance System	189				•	
Survey	189					•
Suspended Solids	189				•	
Swale	189					•
Swimming Pool	190	•				
Syndicate	190					•
Synergism	190					•

— T —

	Page Number	Zoning	Subdivision	Site Plan	Environmental	All
Tailings	190				•	
Taking	190					•
Tank Farm	190	•				
Tavern	190	•				

258

	Page Number	Zoning	Subdivision	Site Plan	Environmental	All
Toxic Pollutants	193				●	
Toxicity	193				●	
Trace Metals	194				●	
Tract	194					●
Tract House	194		●			
Traffic Count	194					●
Traffic Generator	194					●
Trailer	194	●				
Trailer Court	194	●		●		
Transfer Of Development Rights (TDR)	194	●	●	●		
Transition Zone	194	●				
Transitional Area	194	●				
Transitional Care Home	195	●				
Transitional Clinic Care	195	●				
Transitional Use	195	●				
Transportation Services, Accessory	195	●				
Transportation Services, Local	195	●				
Trap	196				●	
Travel Trailer	196	●				
Tree House	196	●				
Trickling Filter	196				●	
Trip	196	●	●	●		
Trip Ends	197	●	●	●		
Trip Generation	197	●	●	●		
Triple Wide Units	198	●				
Triplex	198	●				
Truck Camper	198	●				
Truck Stop	198	●				
Trucking Terminal	199	●				

259

	Page Number	Zoning	Subdivision	Site Plan	Environmental	All
— V —						
Vacancy	201	●				
Vacancy Rate	202	●				
Vacant Land	202	●			●	
Vacation Home	202	●				
Valley	202				●	
Van	203			●		
Vanpooling	203			●		
Vapor	203				●	
Vapor Plume	203				●	
Vaporization	203				●	
Variance	203	●				
Variance, Bulk	203	●				
Variance, Hardship	203	●				
Variance, Lot	204	●	●			
Variance, Use	204	●				
Vegetative Protection	204			●	●	
Vehicle, Motor	204					●
Vehicle, Recreational	204	●				
Vehicular Sales Area	204	●				
Vest Pocket Park	204					●
Vocational School	204	●				
Volatile	204				●	
— W —						
Wading Pool	204	●				
Walkup	205	●				

	Page Number	Zoning	Subdivision	Site Plan	Environmental	All
Walkup Establishment	205	●				
Wall	205					●
Warehouse	205	●				
Warehousing	205	●				
Warehousing, Private	205	●				
Warehousing, Public	205	●				
Waste	205				●	
Wasteland	205				●	
Wastewater	205				●	
Water Bodies	206				●	
Water-Carrying Capacity	206				●	
Water Course	206					●
Water Pollution	206		●	●	●	
Water Quality Criteria	206				●	
Water Quality Standard	206				●	
Water Rights	206			●	●	
Water Supply System	206				●	
Water Table	207			●	●	
Water Transportation	207	●				
Waterfront Property	207					●
Watershed	207				●	
Wetlands	207					●
Wholesale Trade	207	●				

— Y —

	Page Number	Zoning	Subdivision	Site Plan	Environmental	All
Yard	207	●		●	●	
Yard Depth	208	●		●	●	
Yard, Front	208	●		●	●	
Yard Line	208	●		●	●	

	Page Number	Zoning	Subdivision	Site Plan	Environmental	All
Yard, Rear	208		●	●	●	
Yard, Required	208		●	●	●	
Yard, Side	208		●	●	●	
Youth Camp	208		●			

— Z —

	Page Number	Zoning	Subdivision	Site Plan	Environmental	All
Zero Lot Line	209		●			
Zone	209		●			
Zoning	209		●			
Zoning Board	209		●			
Zoning District	209		●			
Zoning Envelope	209		●			
Zoning Map	209		●			
Zoning Officer	209					●
Zoning Permit	209		●			

CENTER
FOR URBAN
POLICY RESEARCH

Coping with the 80s

SHOPPING CENTERS: U.S.A.

by George Sternlieb and James W. Hughes

What is the future of shopping centers? Is there a place for them in the central city? Is the new "middle market" thrust enough to sustain the industry? Or are we overbuilt? The pick of the consultants, developers, financiers, and merchants of the field give their answers.

Hardcover, 256 pp. $17.95
ISBN: 0-88285-068-7

ENERGY FORECASTING FOR PLANNERS: TRANSPORTATION MODELS

by W. Patrick Beaton and J.H. Weyland

The best fully documented and tested fuel consumption forecasting models are presented in a clear, easy-to-follow text. Complete with full examples.

Hardcover, 250 pp. 35 Exhibits. $17.95
ISBN: 0-88285-071-7

THE ADAPTIVE REUSE HANDBOOK: PROCEDURES TO INVENTORY, CONTROL, MANAGE, AND REEMPLOY SURPLUS MUNICIPAL PROPERTIES

by Robert W. Burchell and David Listokin

The basic handbook for *all* municipal realty officials and developers in U.S. cities. Includes practical approaches from the field.

Hardcover, 576 pp. 150 Exhibits. $28.50
ISBN 0-88285-066-0

ENERGY AND LAND USE

by Robert W. Burchell and David Listokin

The most comprehensive collection of specially written papers on this vital subject. From future land use patterns to measures to conserve energy in development—this is the basic work.

Hardcover, 560 pp. $25.00
ISBN: 0-88285-069-5

THE NEW SUBURBANITES: RACE AND HOUSING IN THE SUBURBS

by Robert W. Lake

Blacks as well as whites are looking for the suburban dream house. How is the process working in real life? Data based on more than 1,000 interviews provide a basis for the analysis.

Hardcover, 256 pp. 50 Exhibits. $17.95
ISBN: 0-88285-072-5

CITIES UNDER STRESS: THE FISCAL CRISIS OF URBAN AMERICA

by Robert W. Burchell and David Listokin

Thirty top urban affairs and municipal finance experts focus on the issues and answers to the major financial problems facing cities in the 1980s.

Hardcover, 704 pp. 204 Exhibits. $28.50
ISBN: 0-88285-064-4

For a full catalogue of CUPR publications, write to:

The Center for Urban Policy Research
Rutgers University—Bldg. 4051
Kilmer Campus
New Brunswick, New Jersey 08903